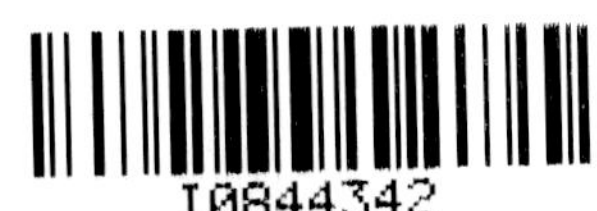

Birds & Flowers

COLORING BOOK FOR ADULTS

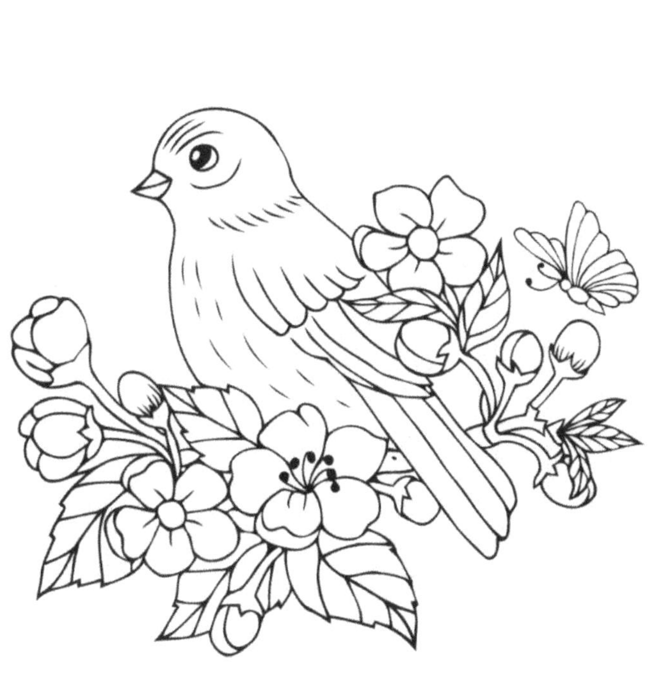

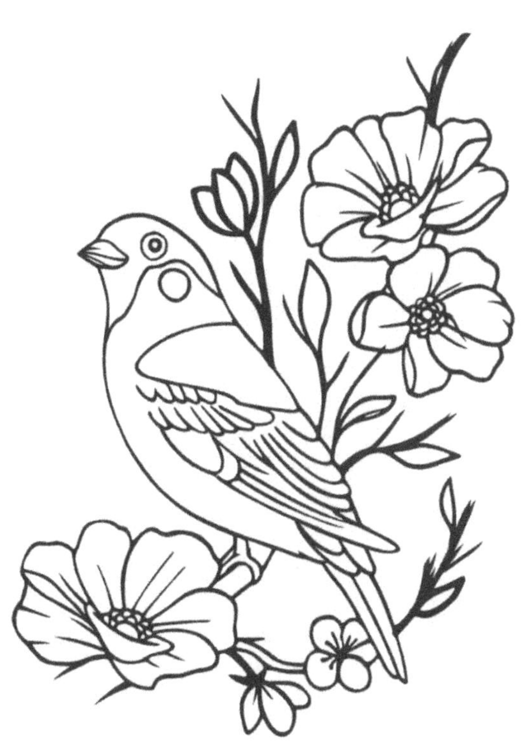

THIS BOOK BELONGS TO.

....

....

....

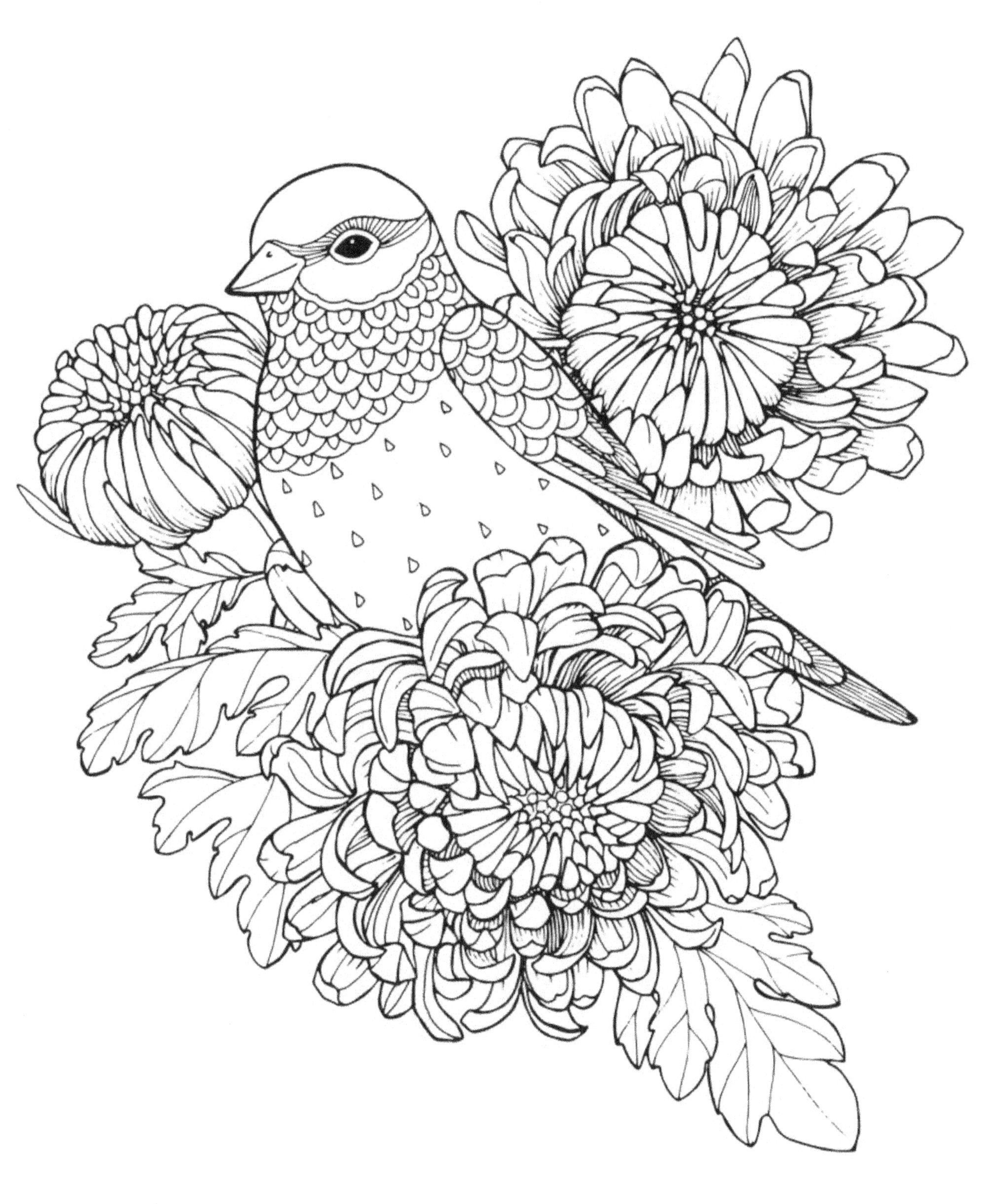

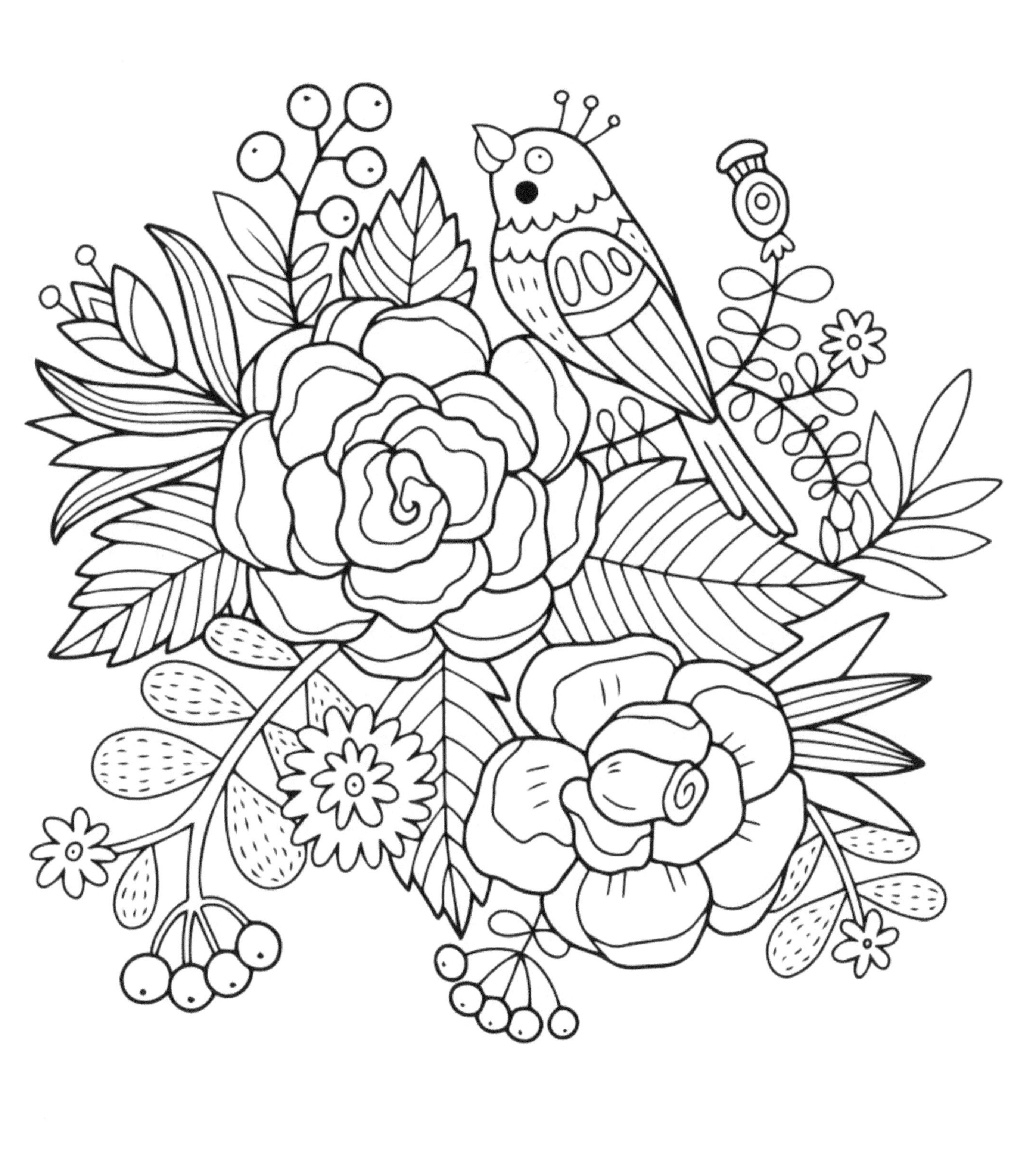

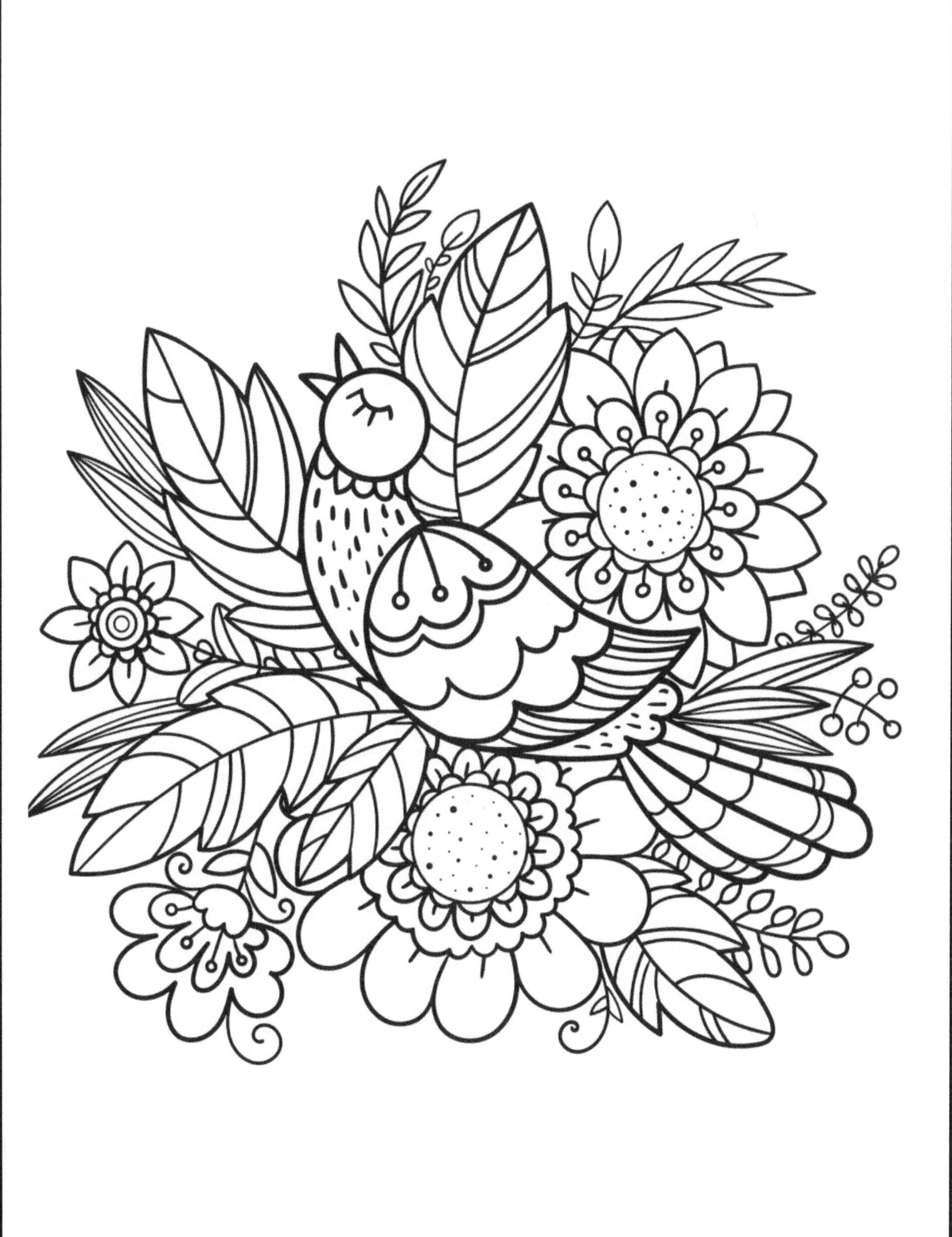

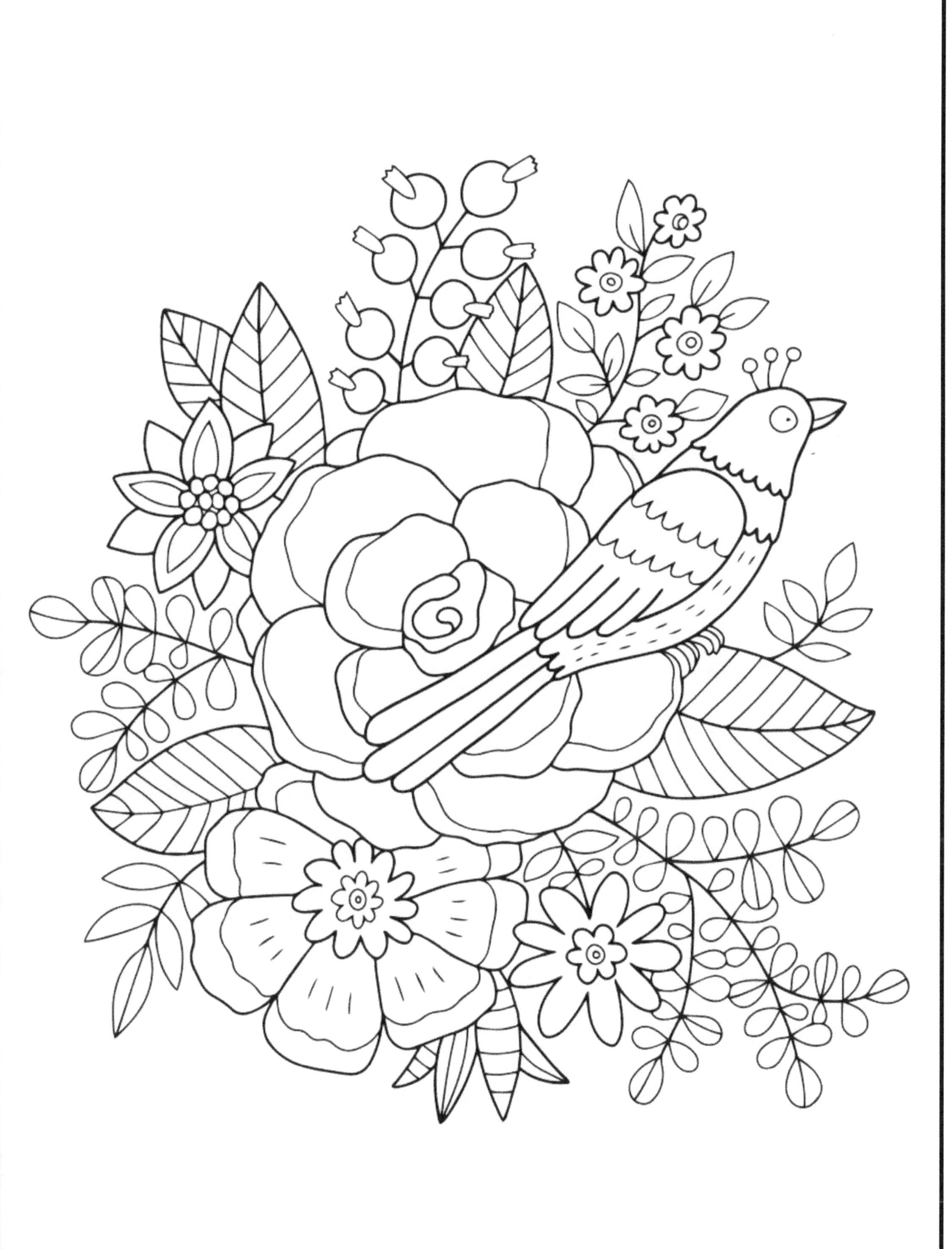

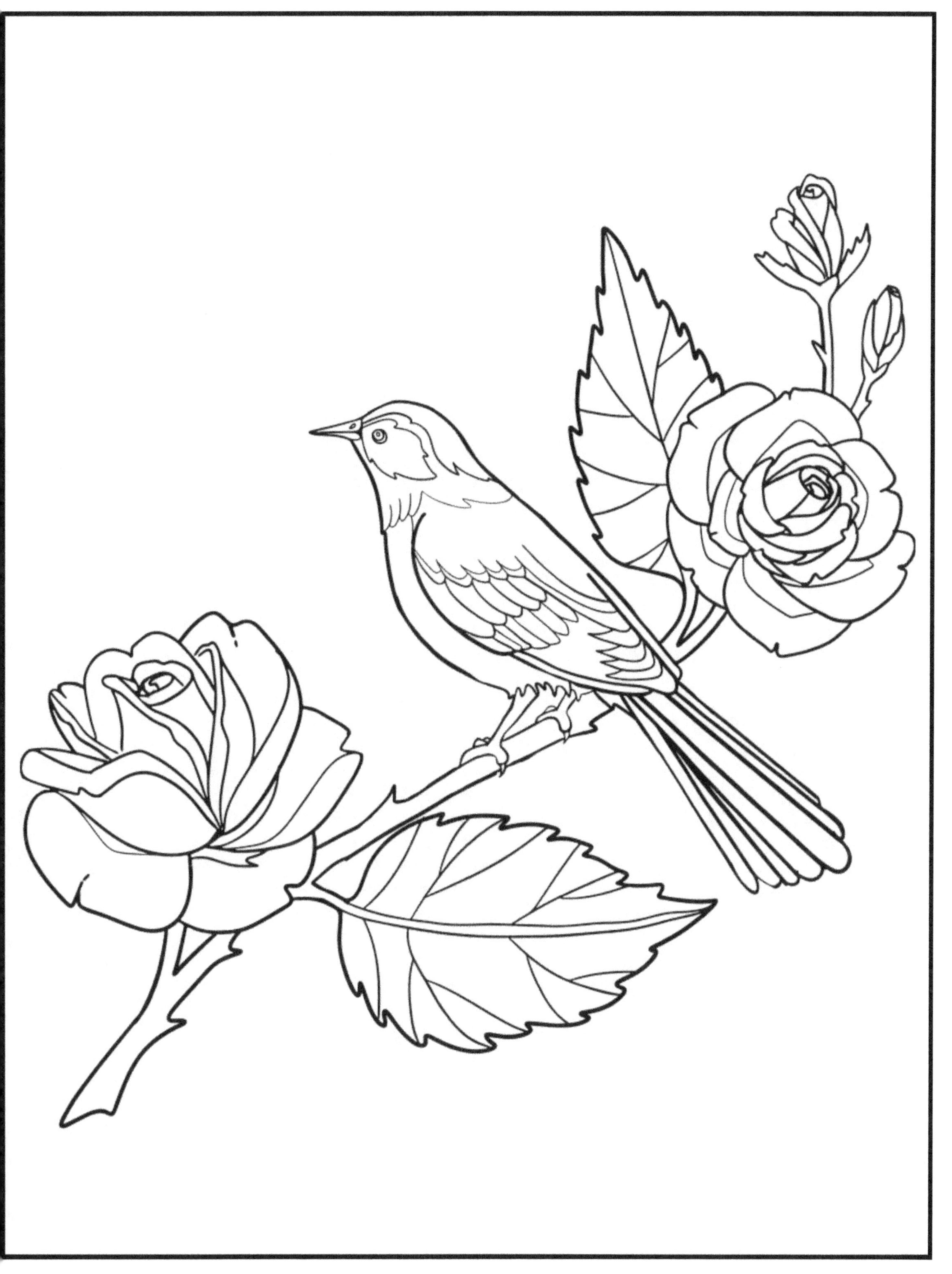

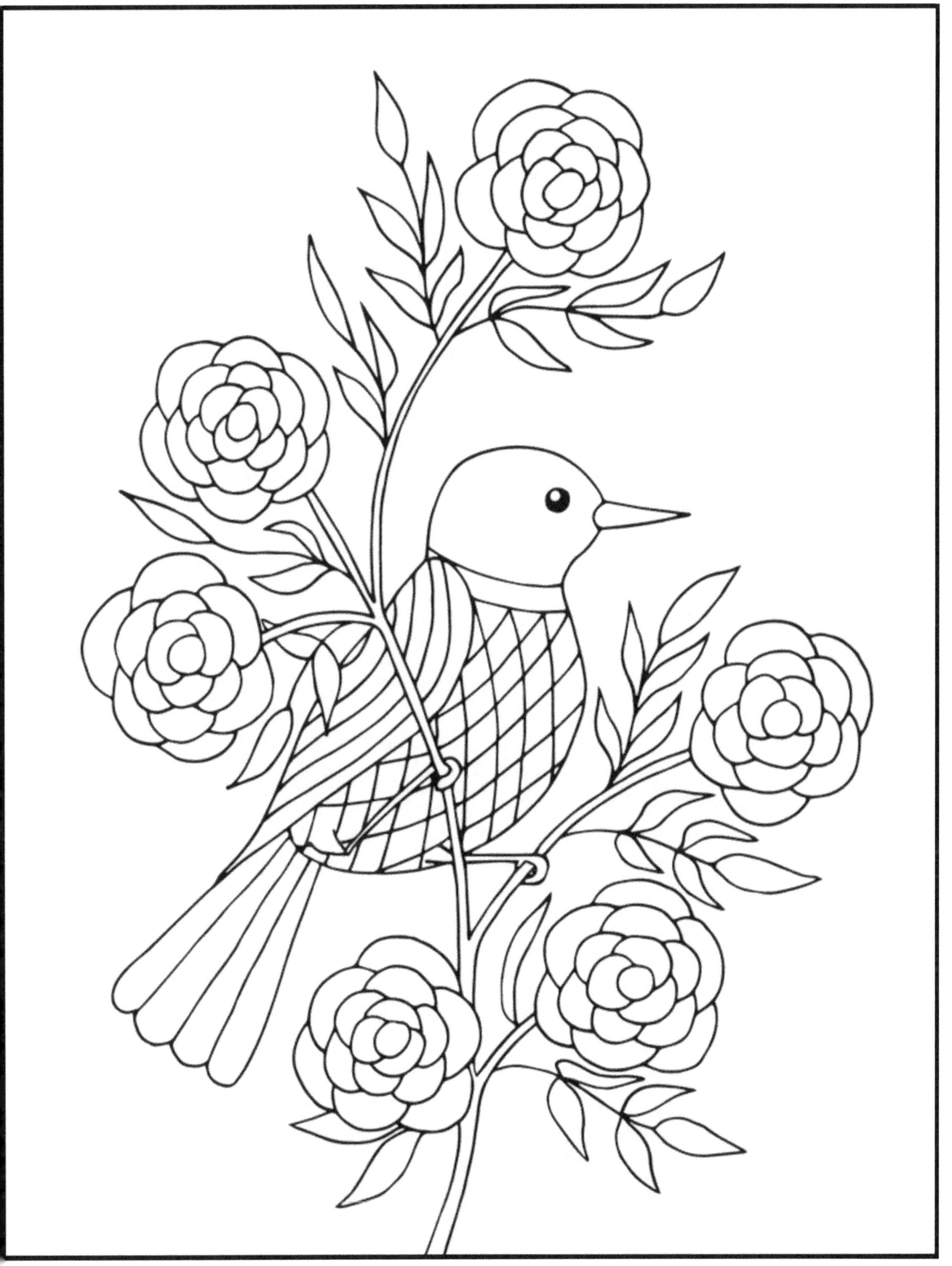

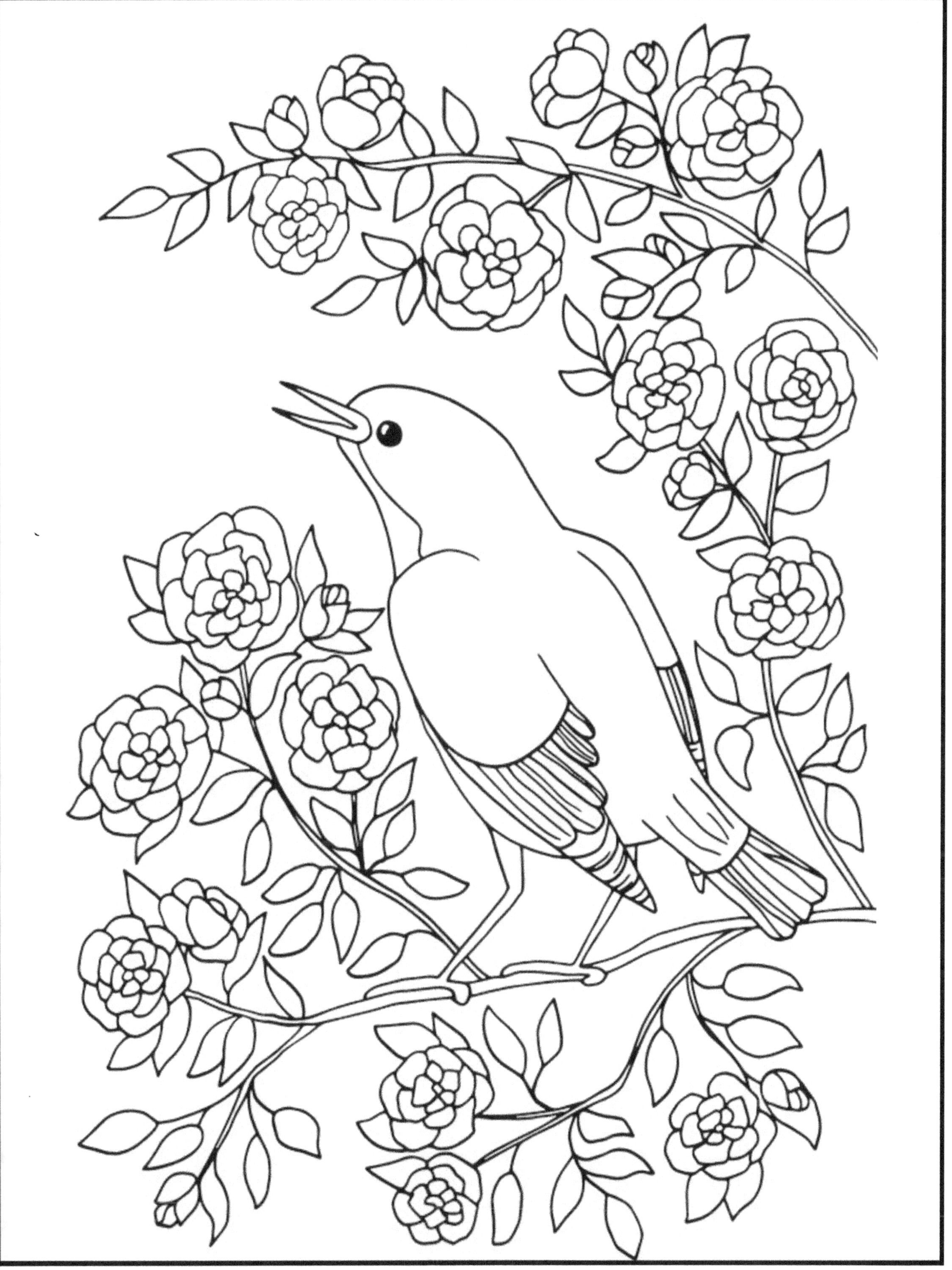

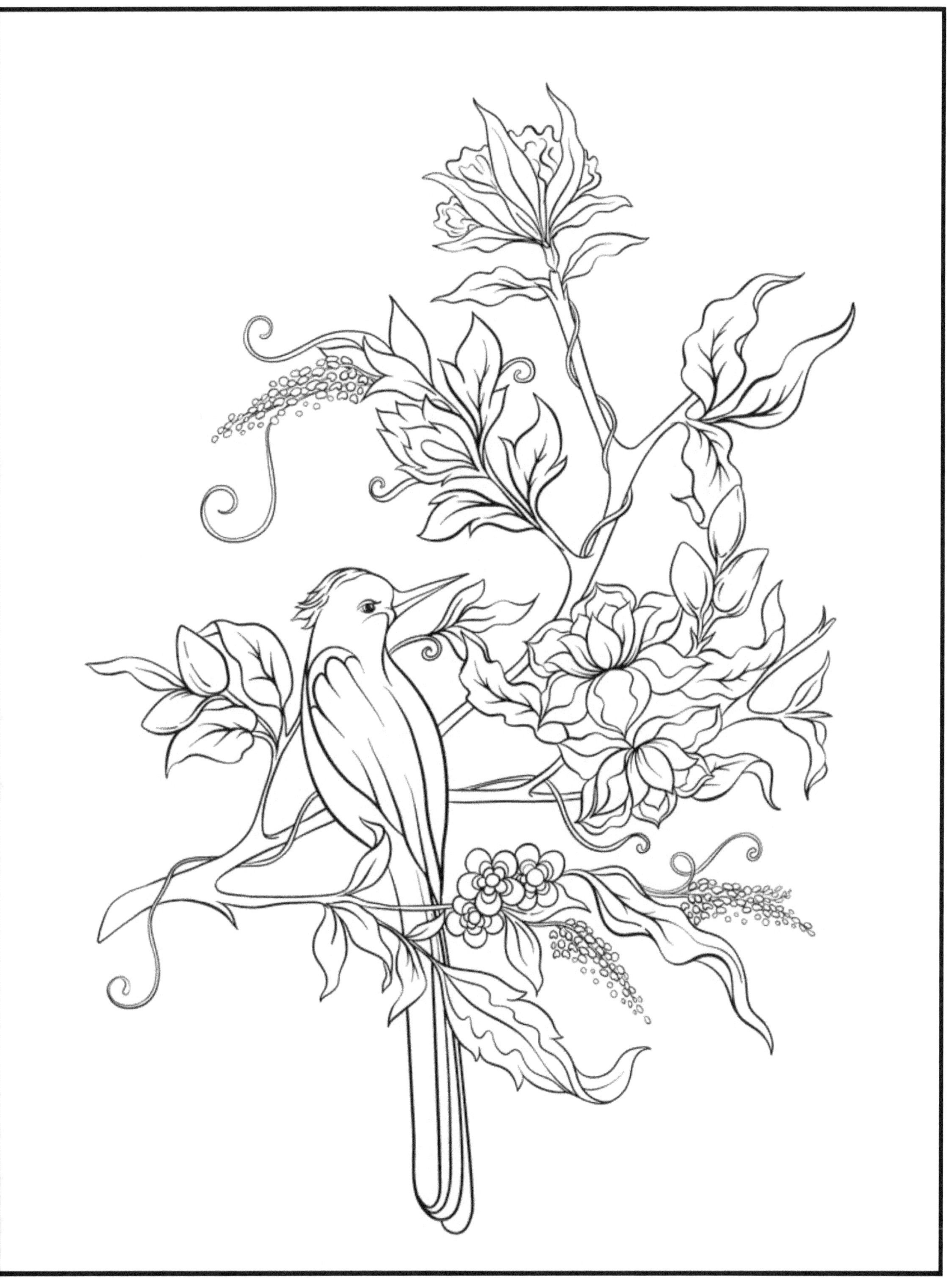

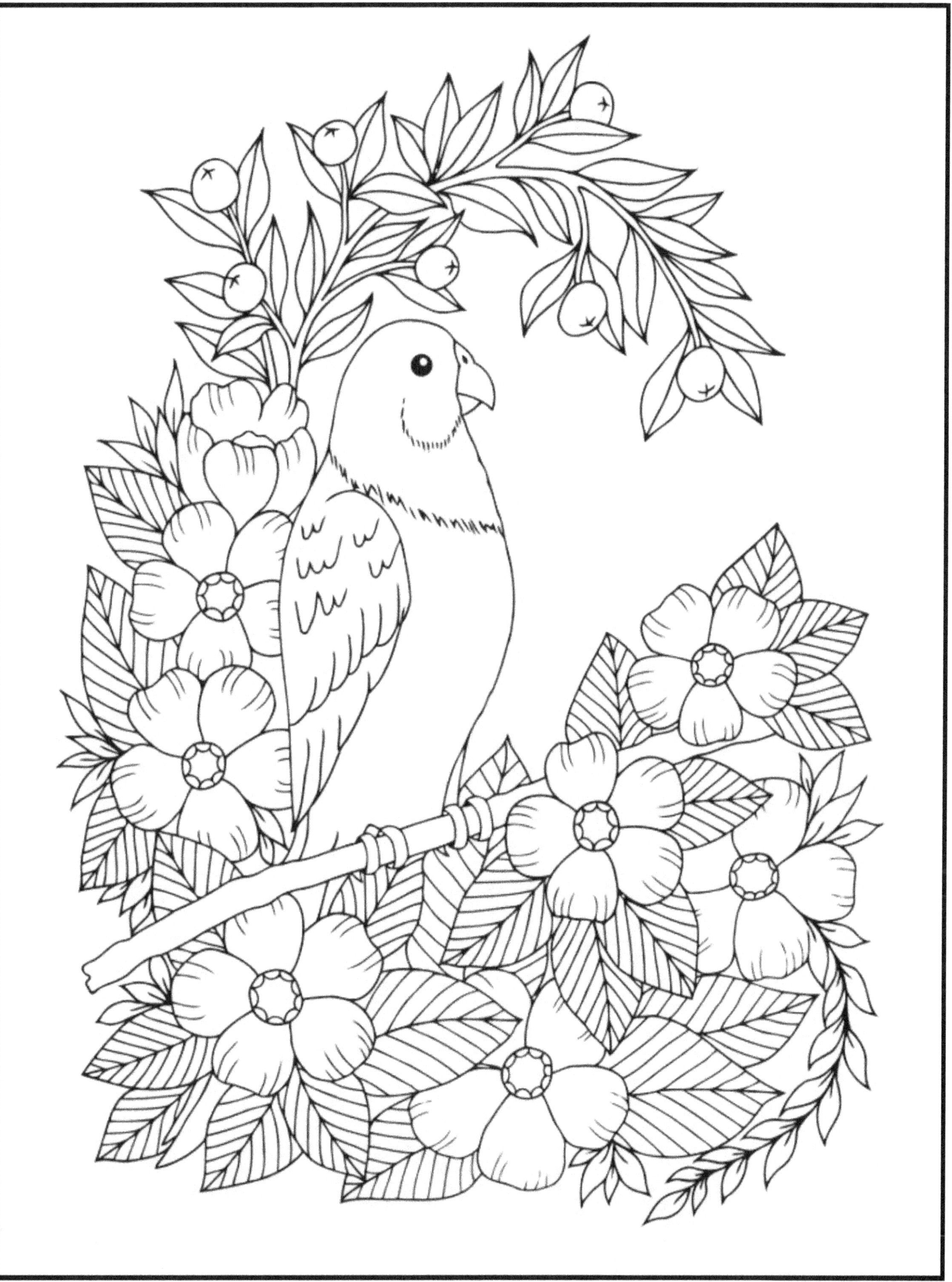

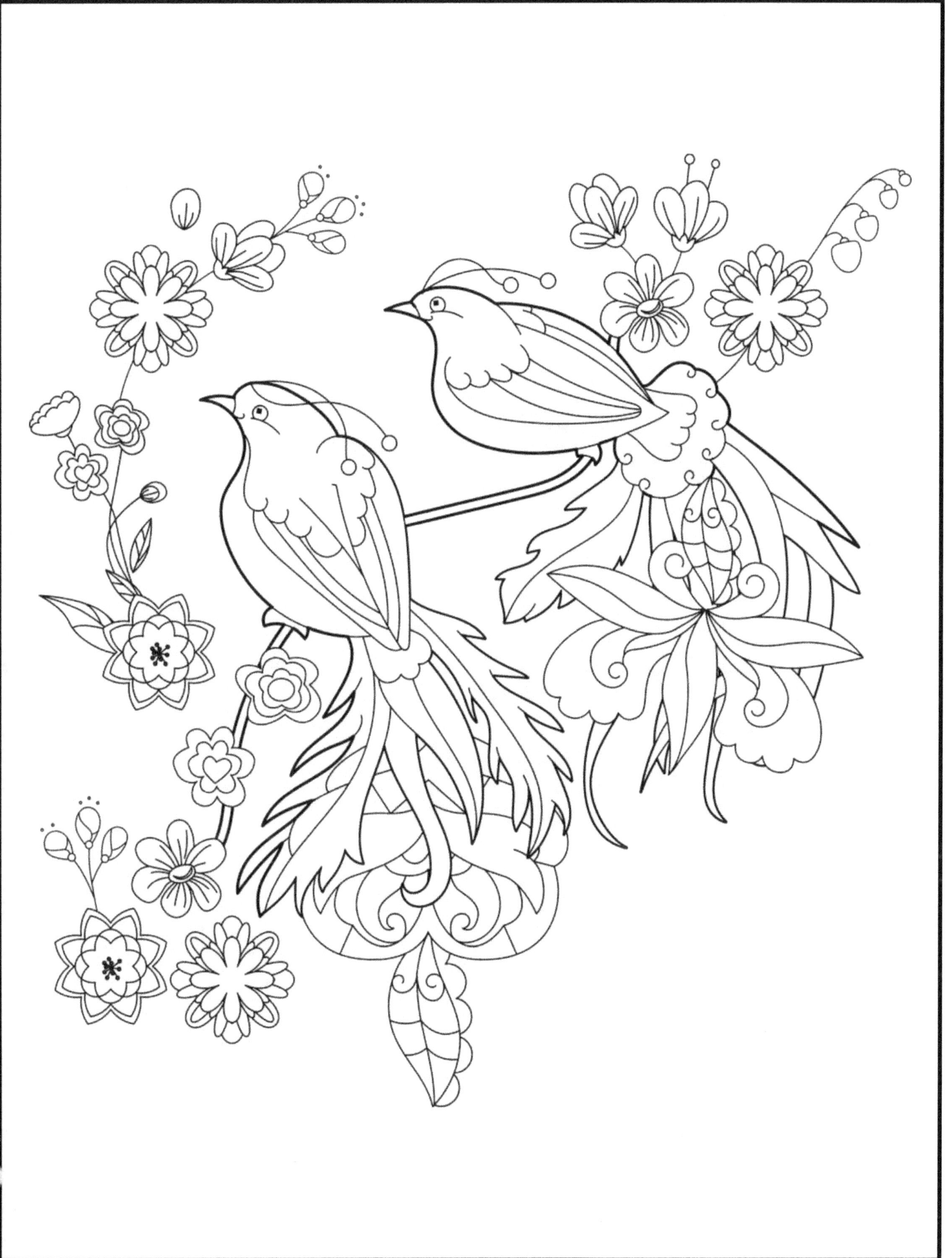

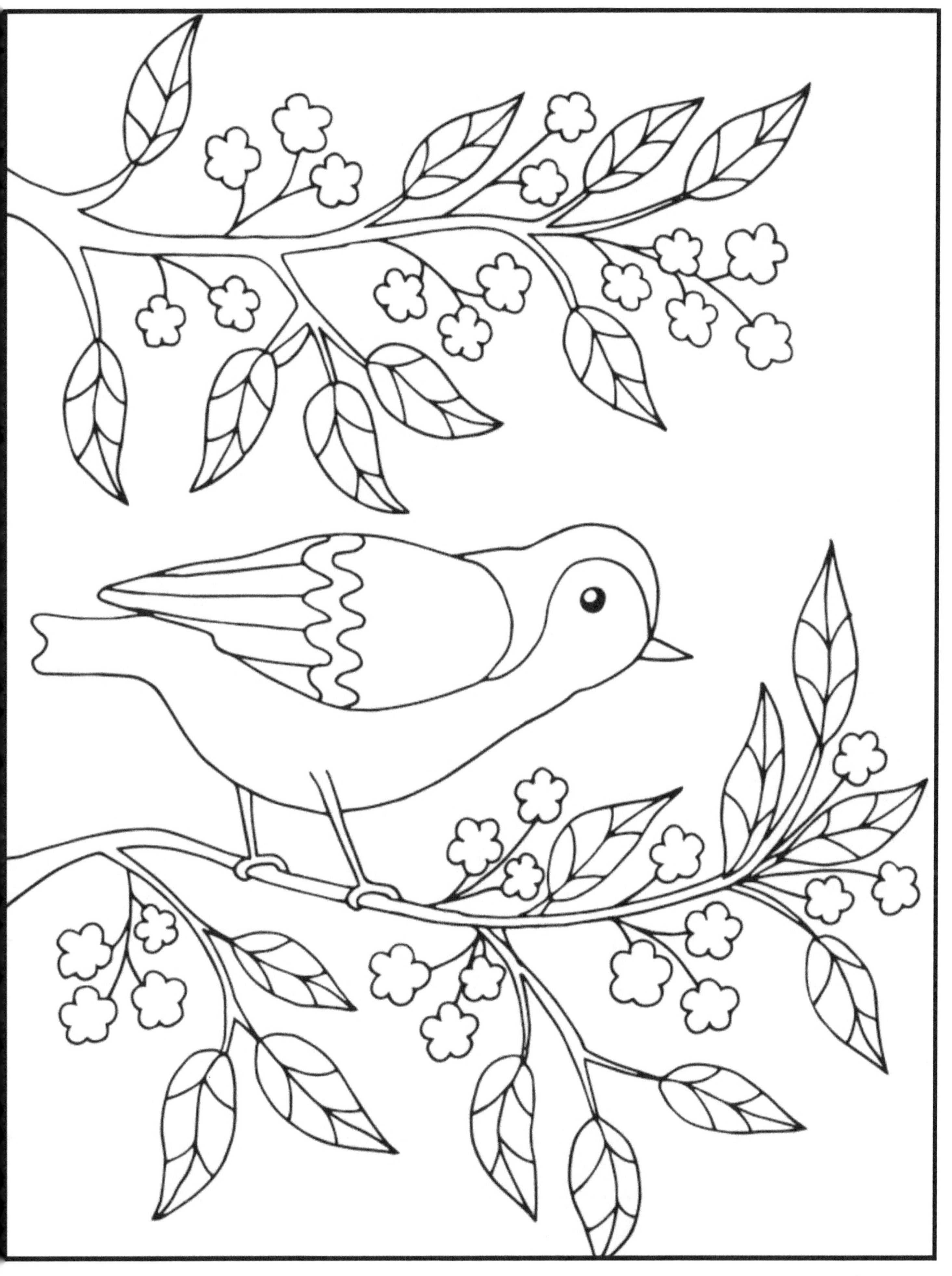

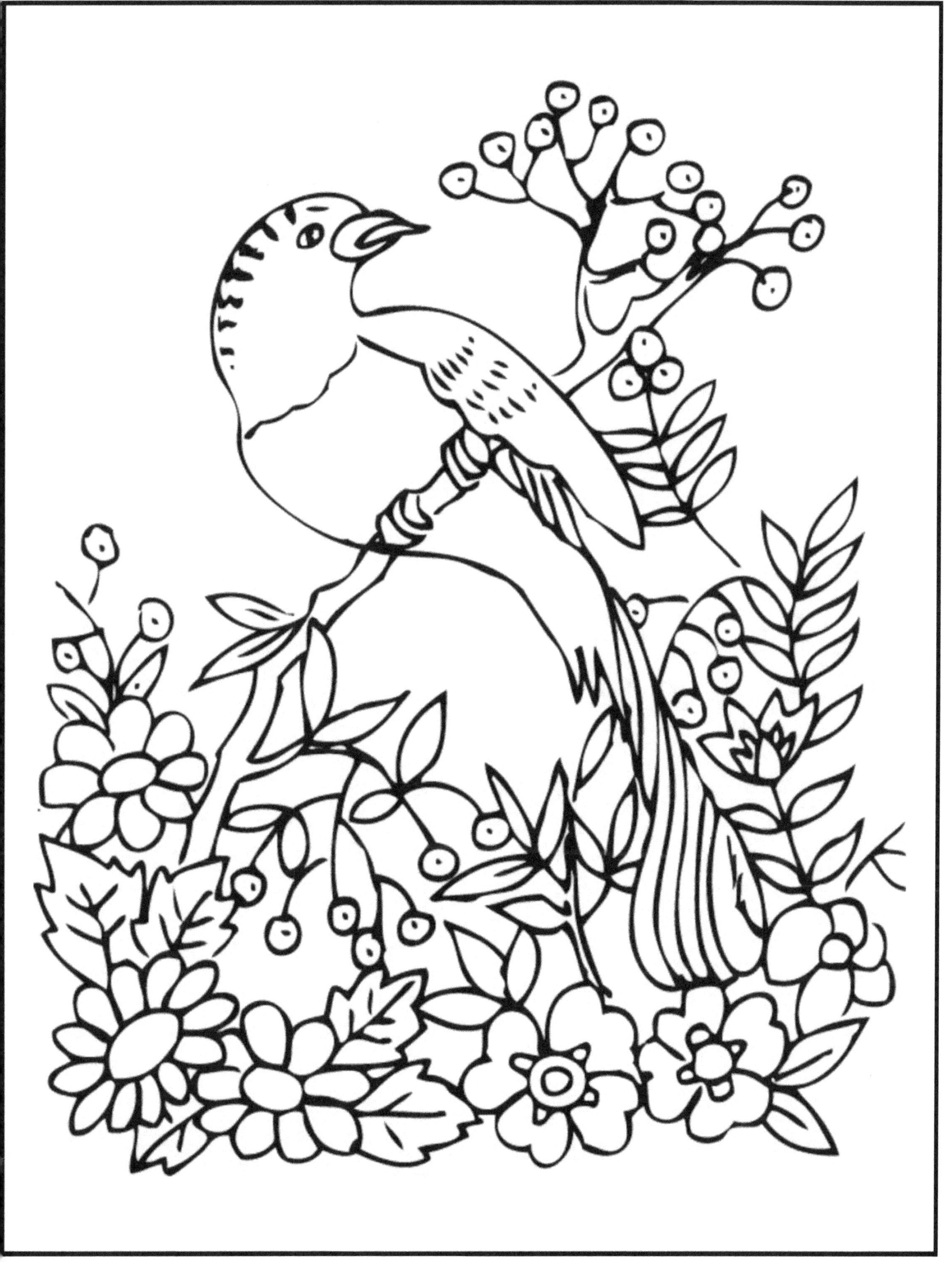

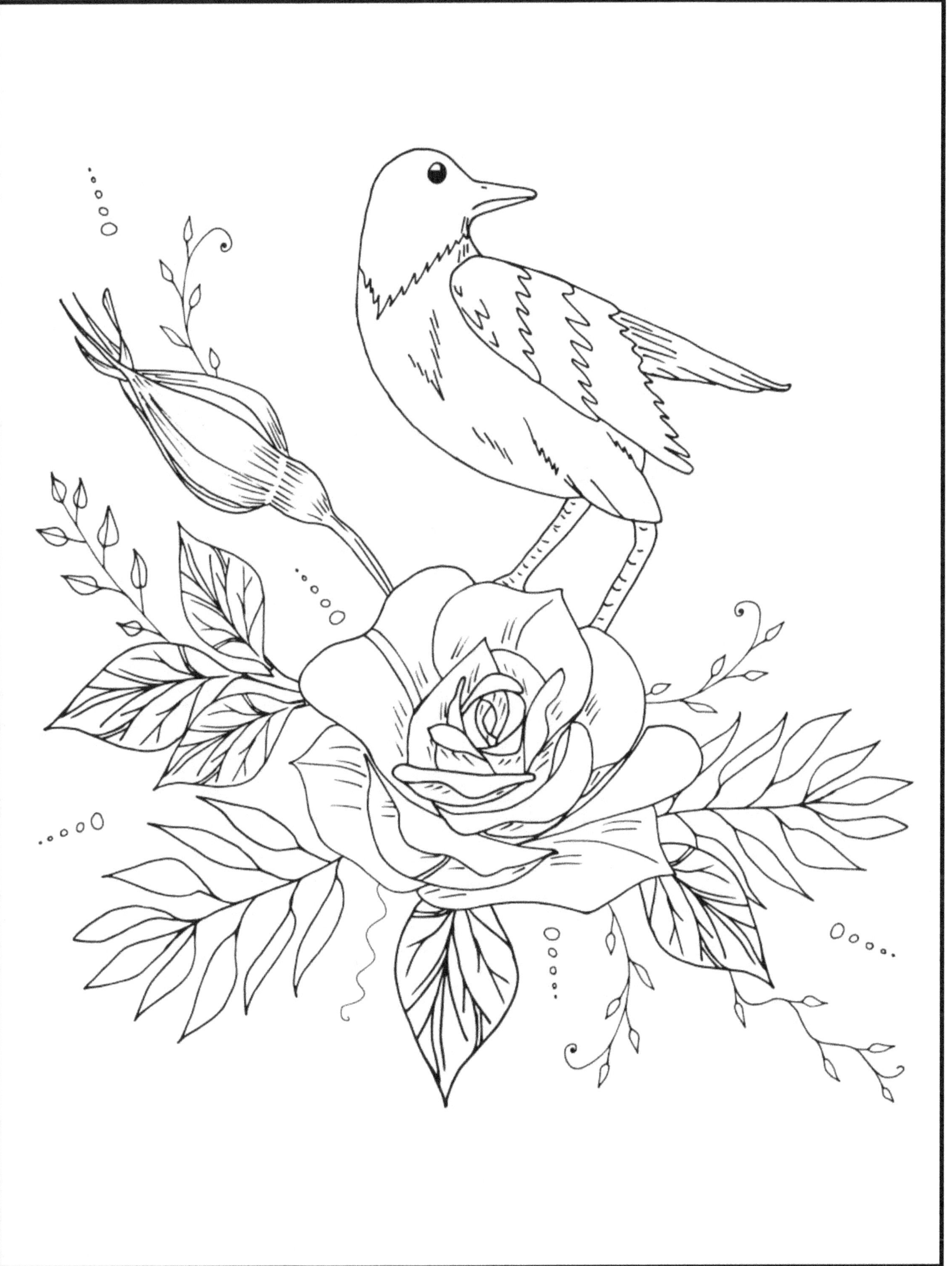

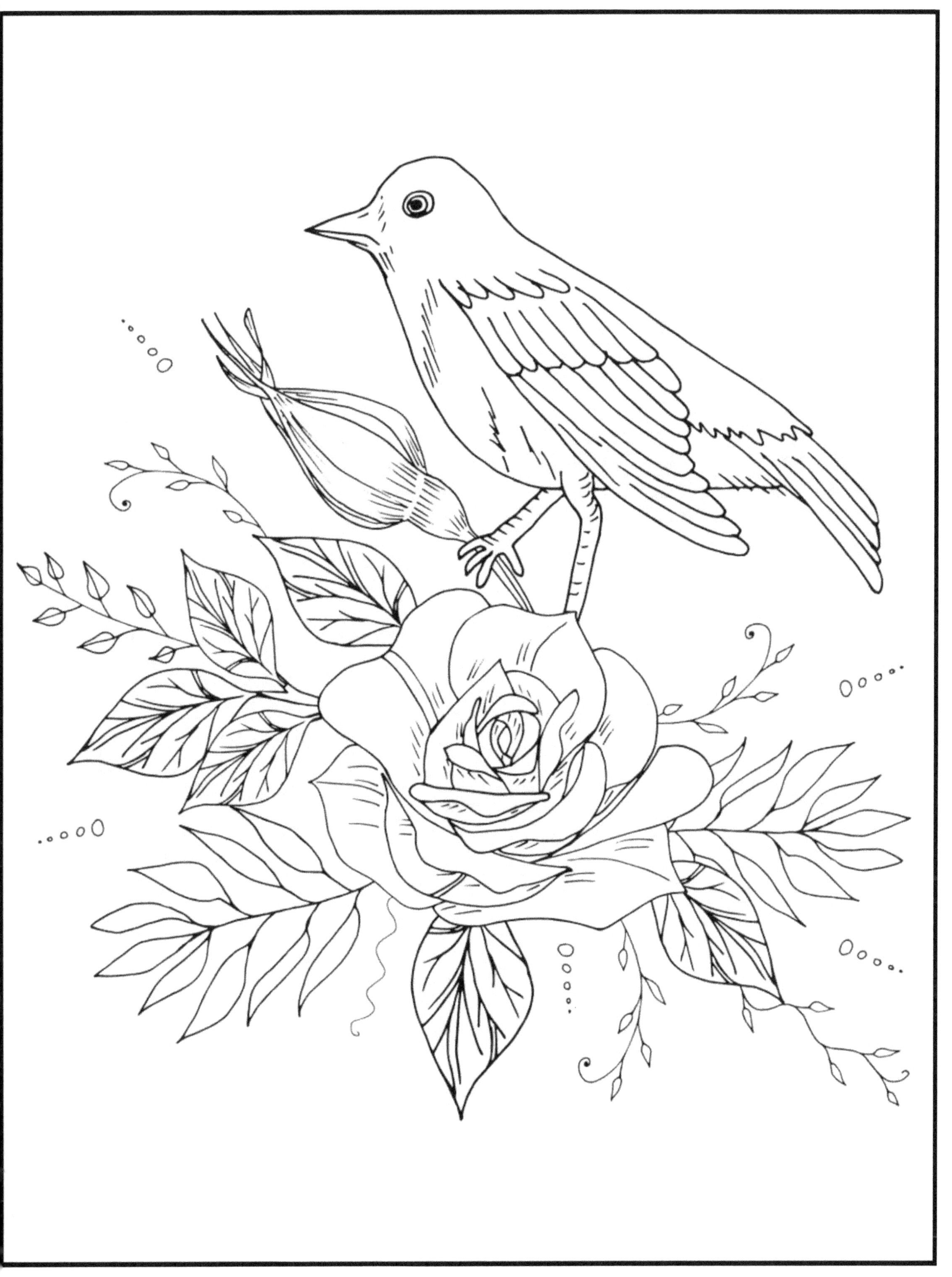

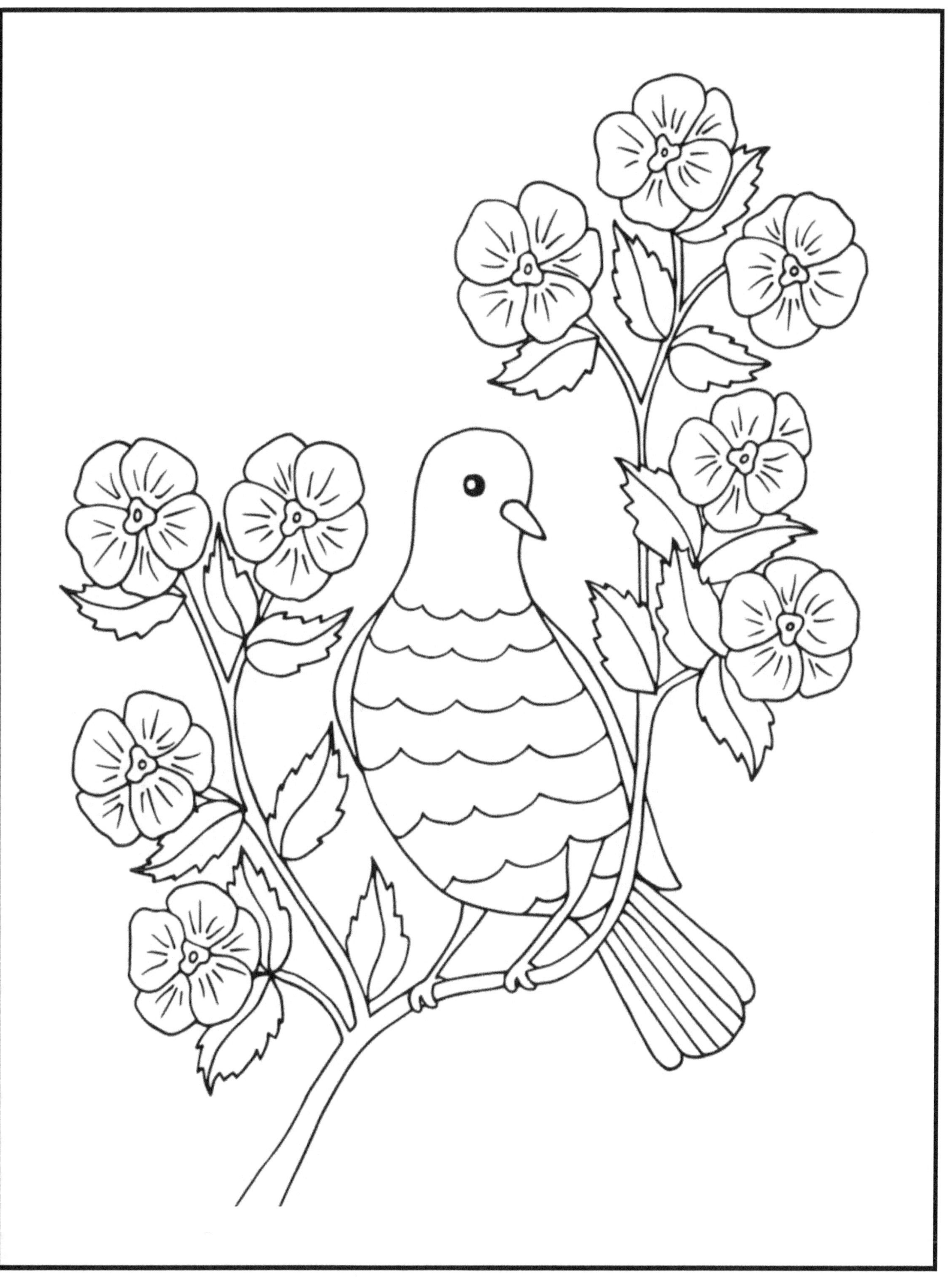

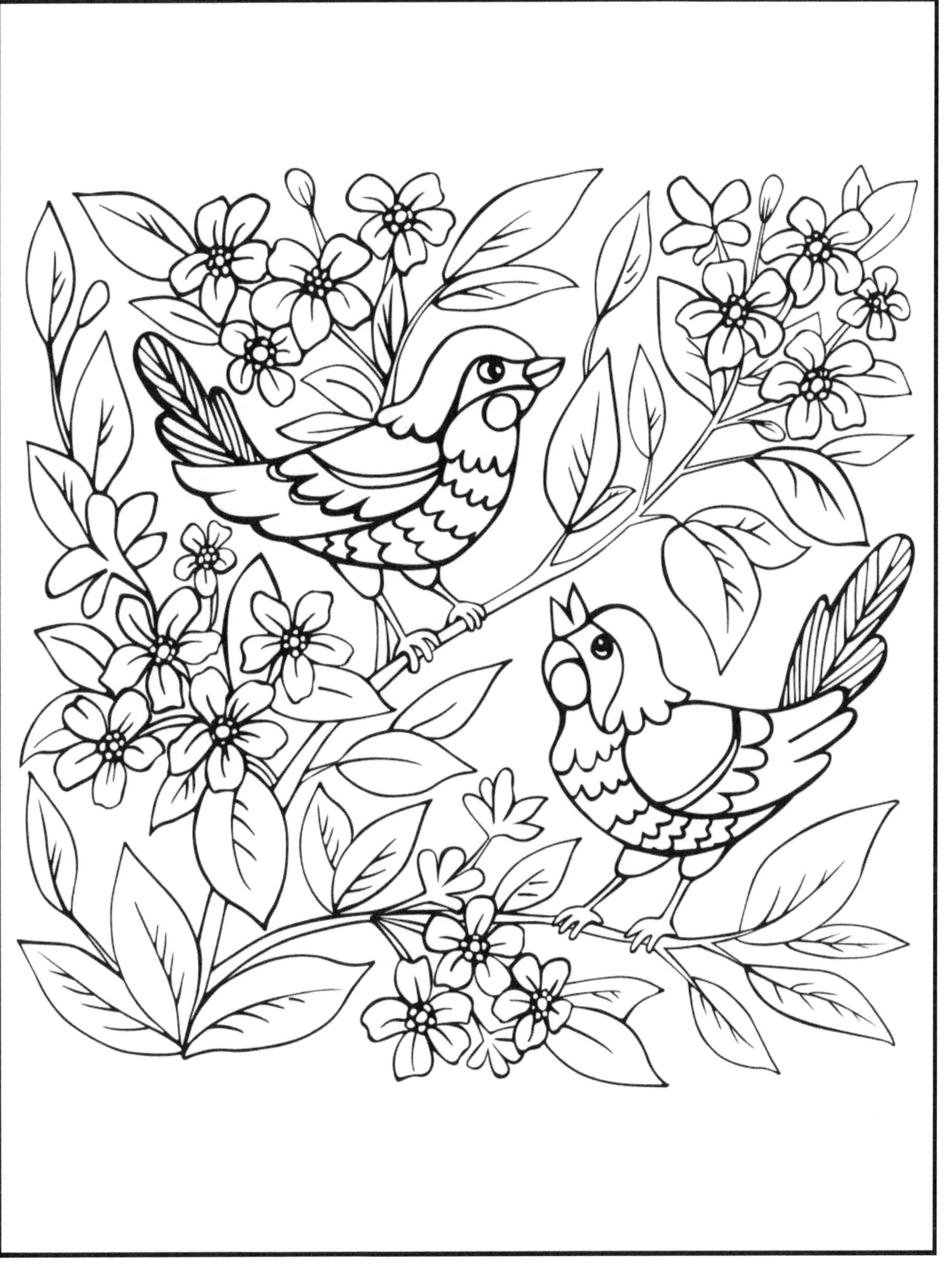

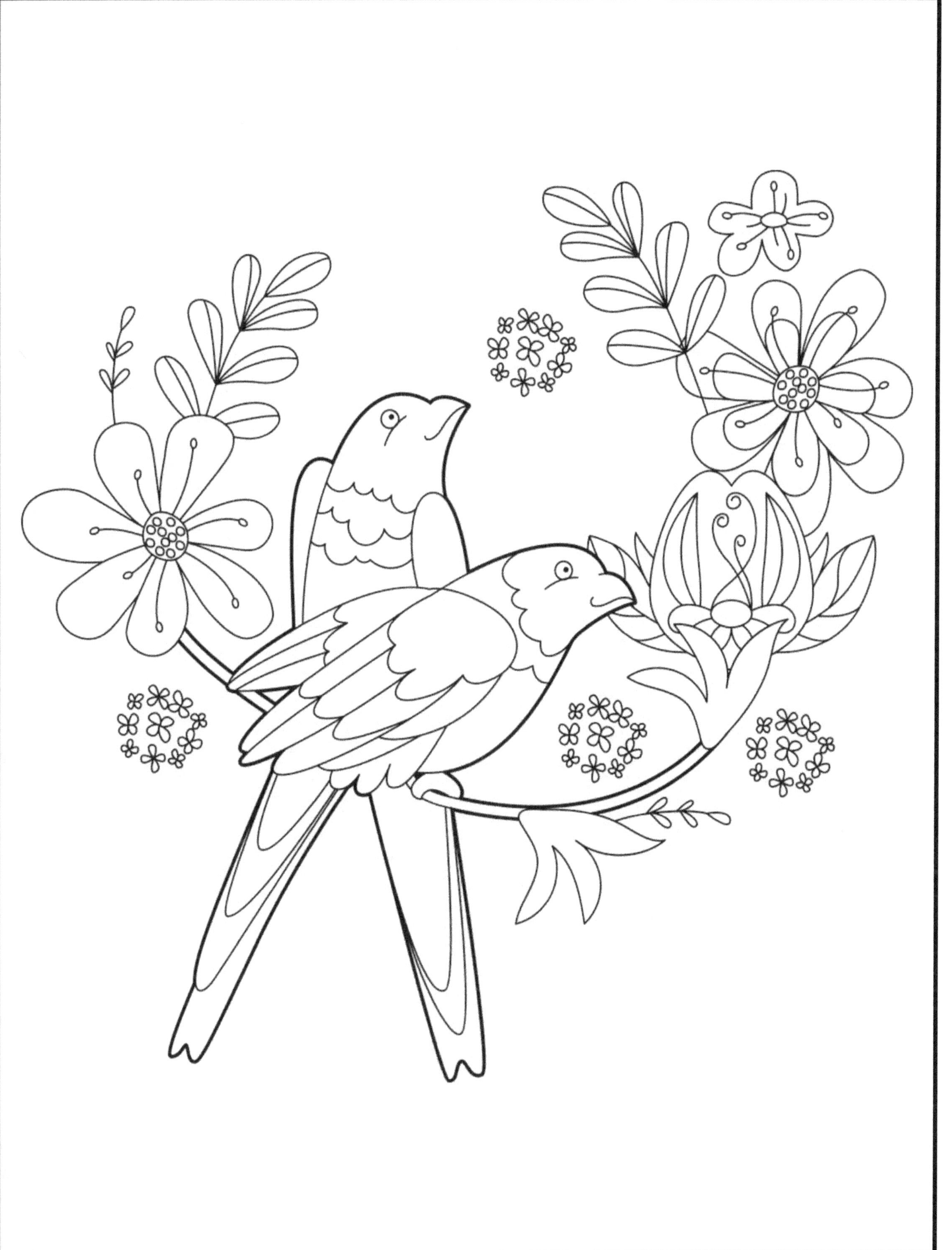

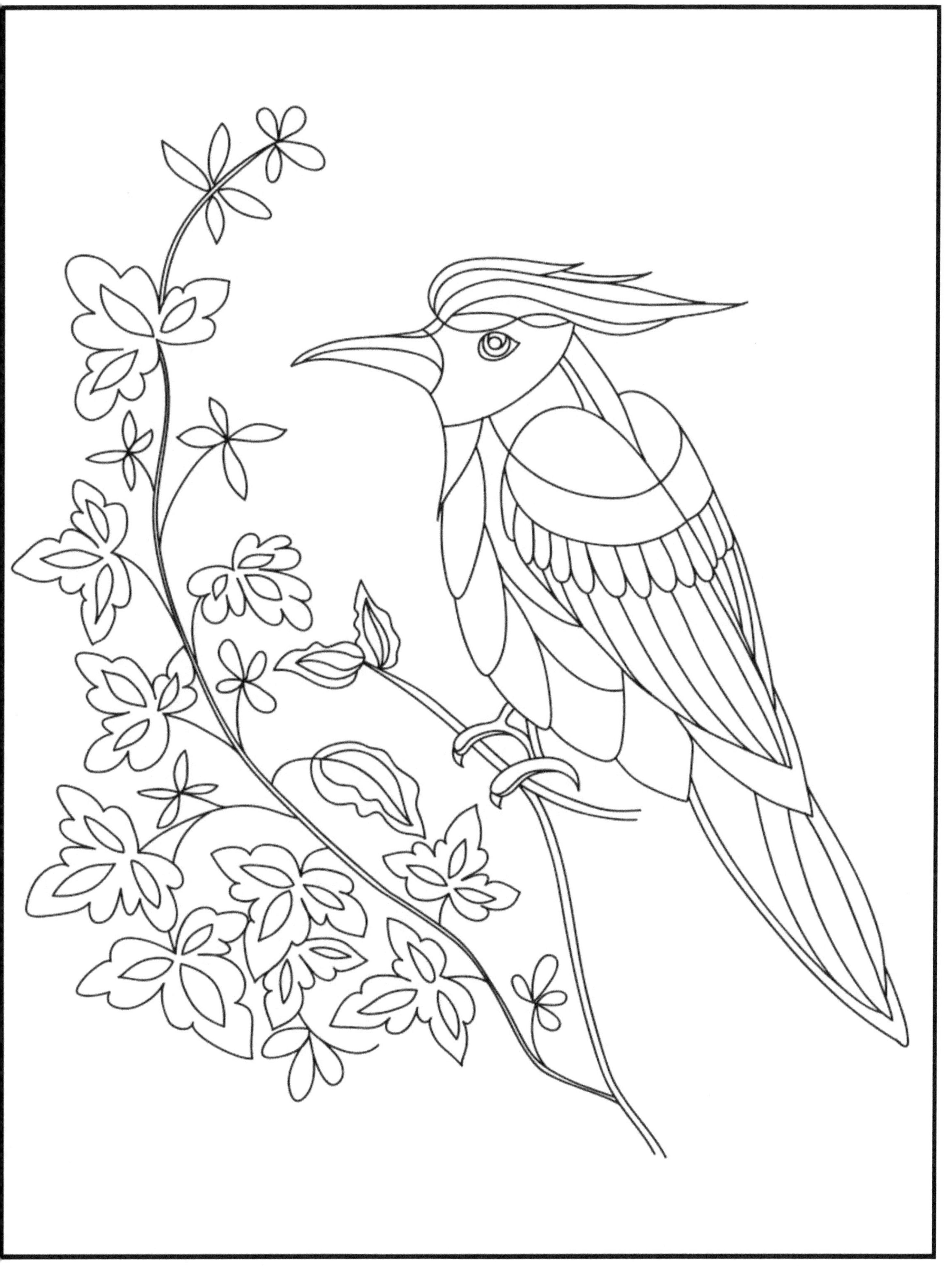

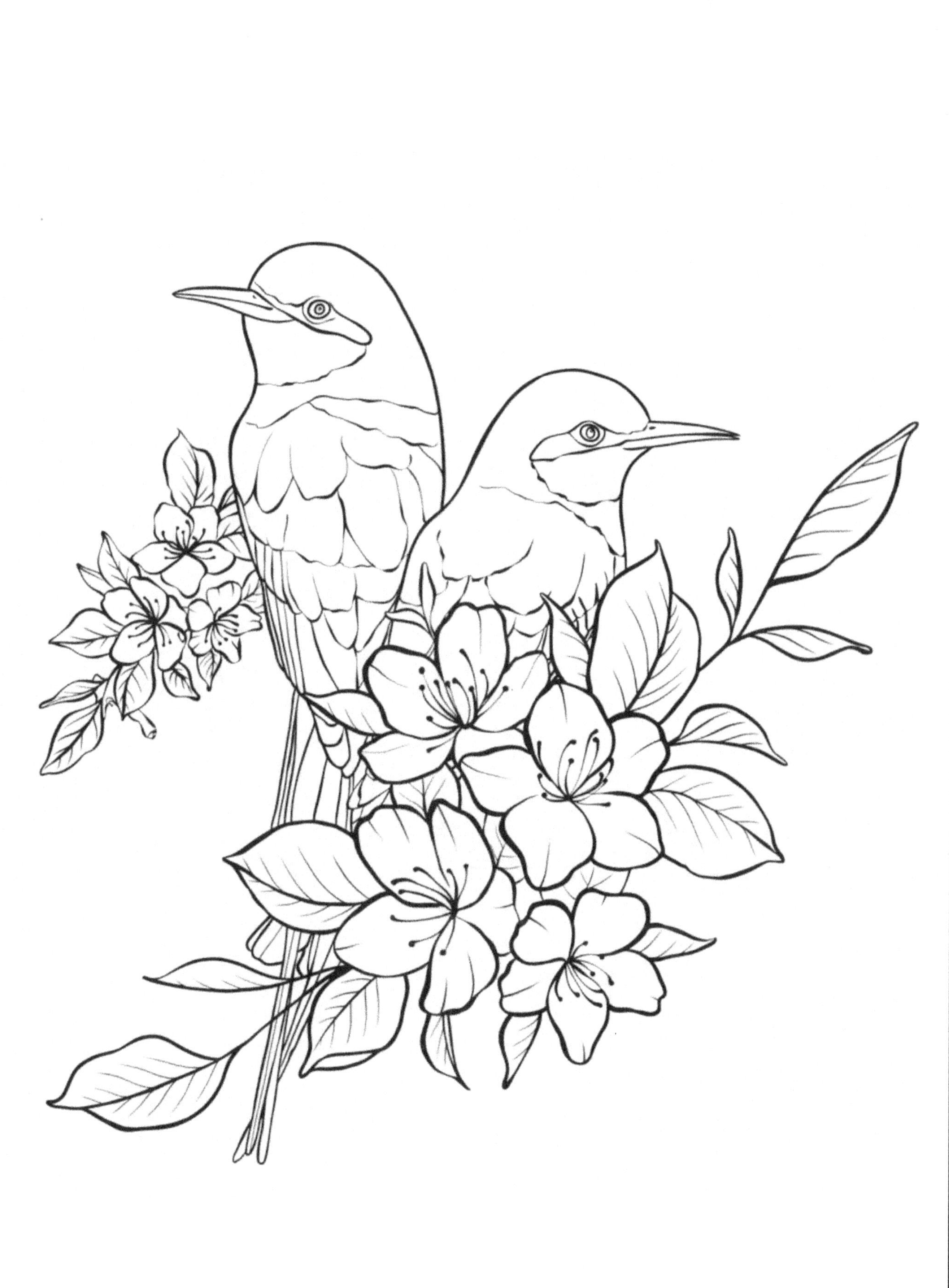

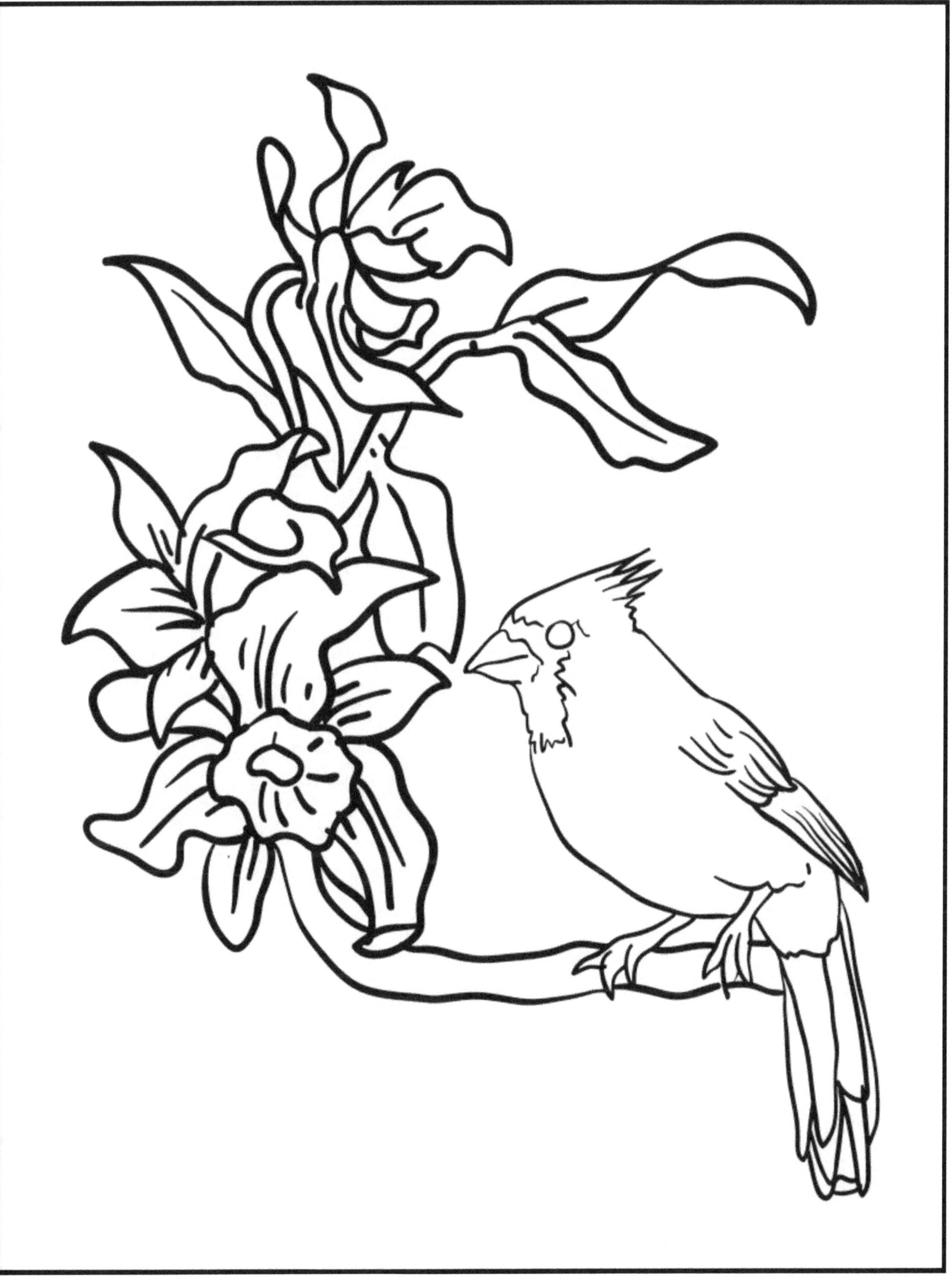

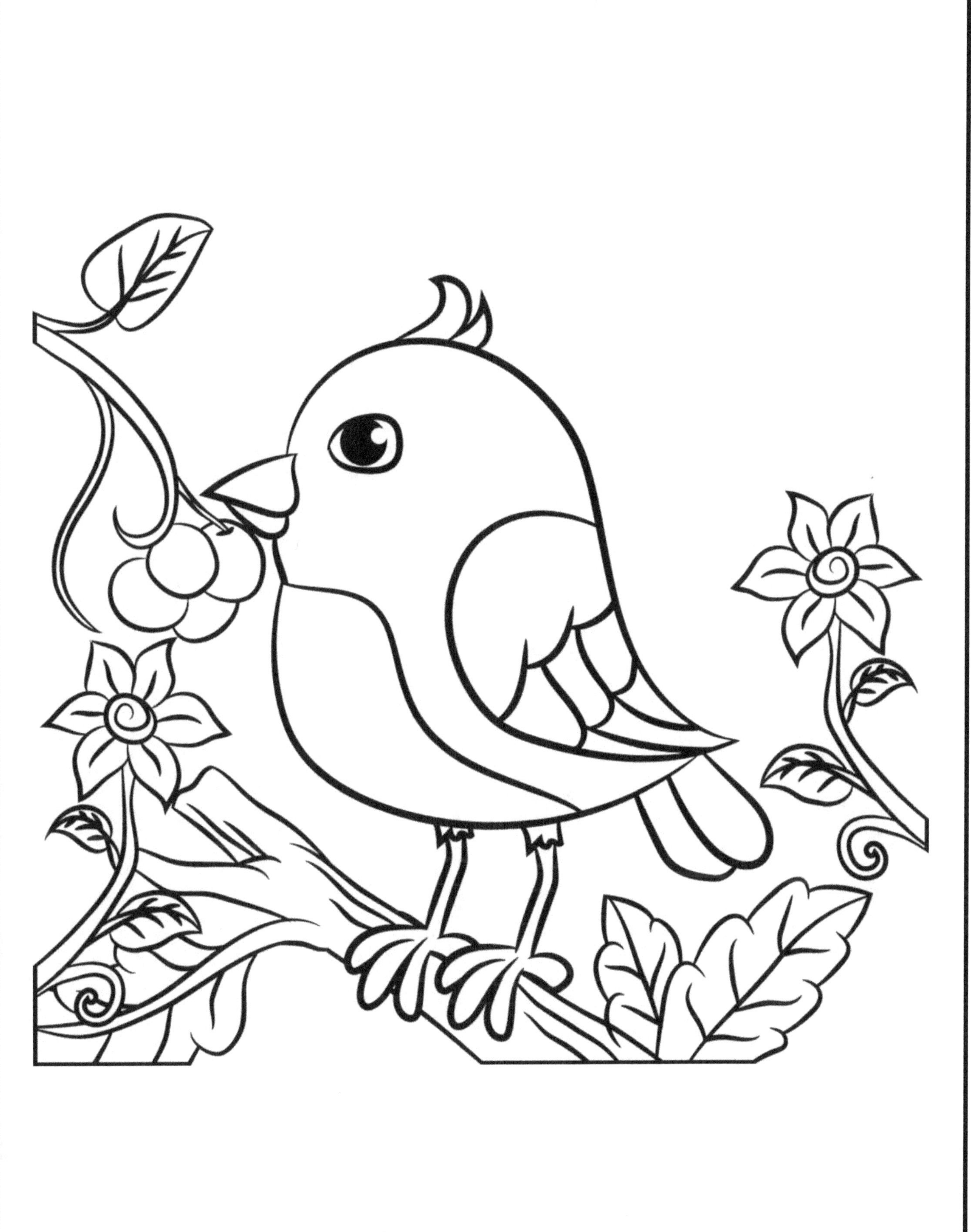

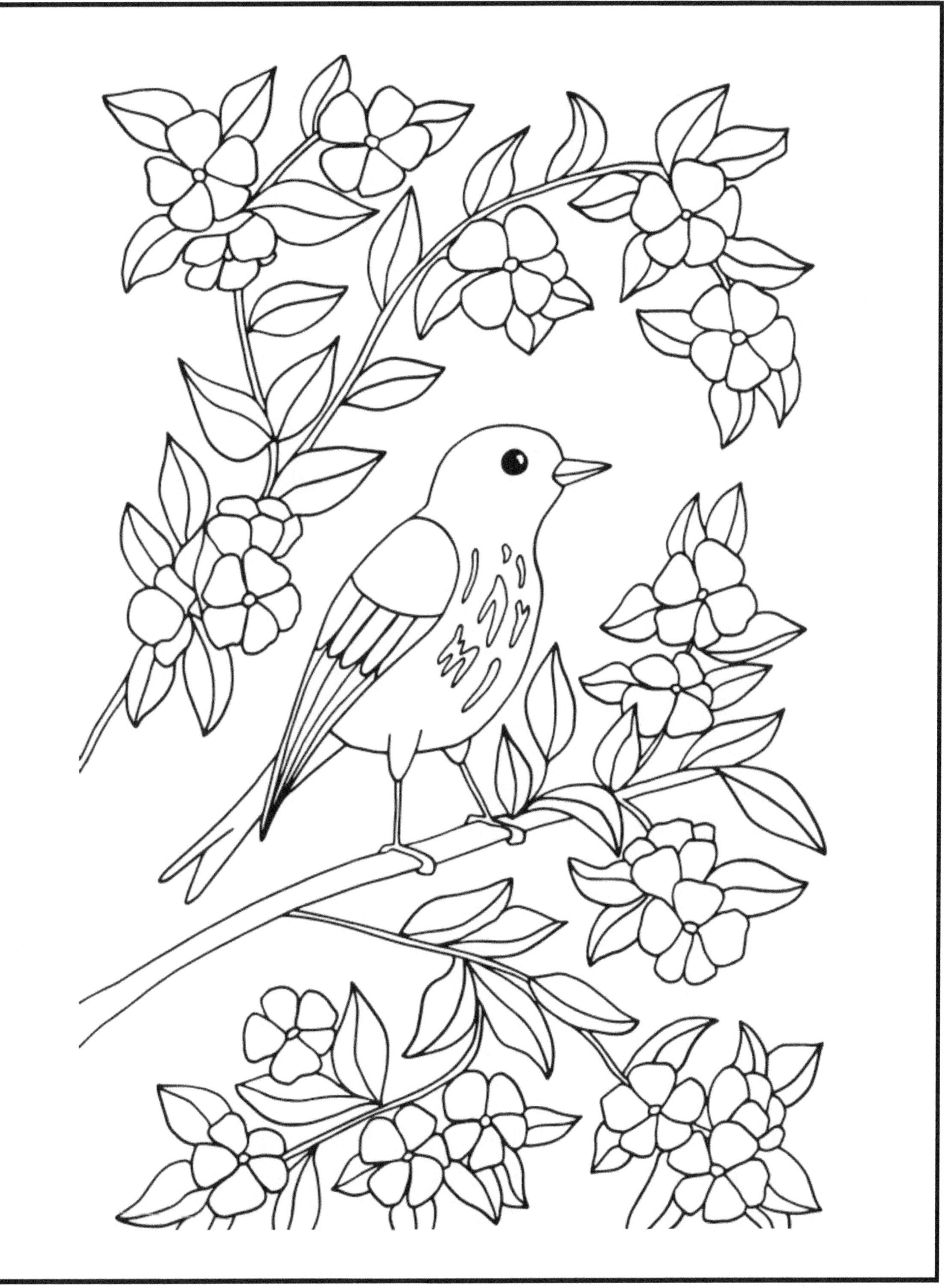

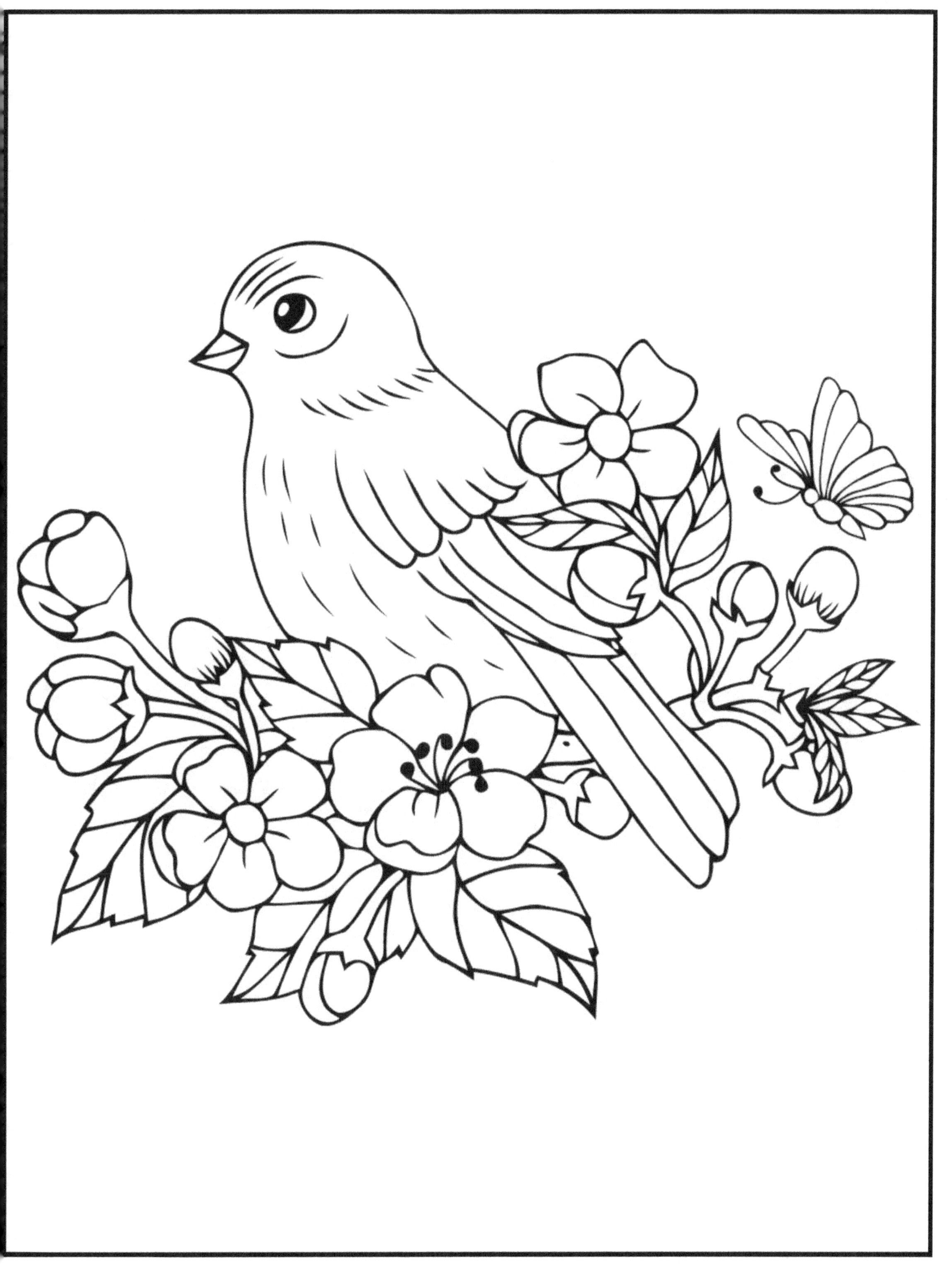

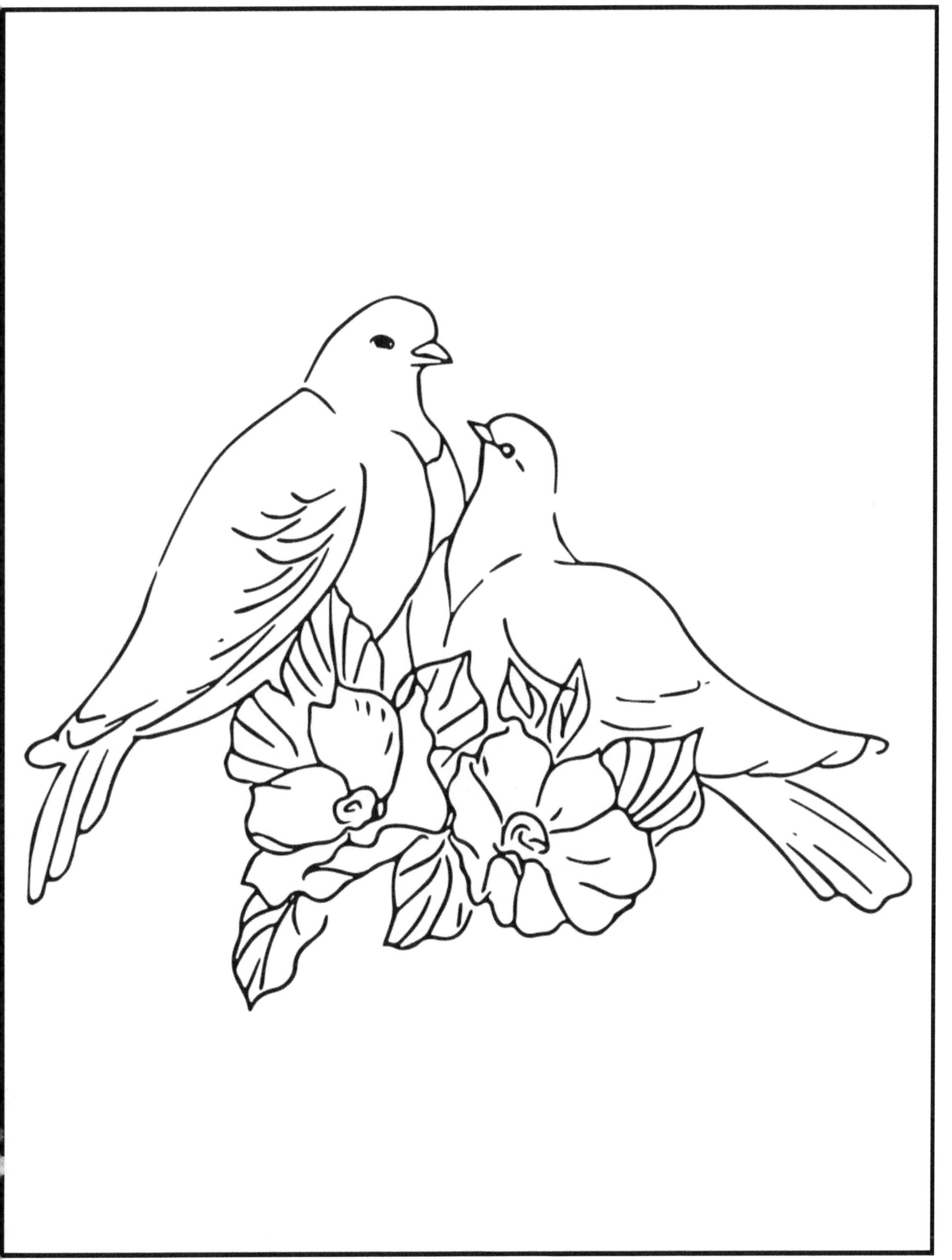

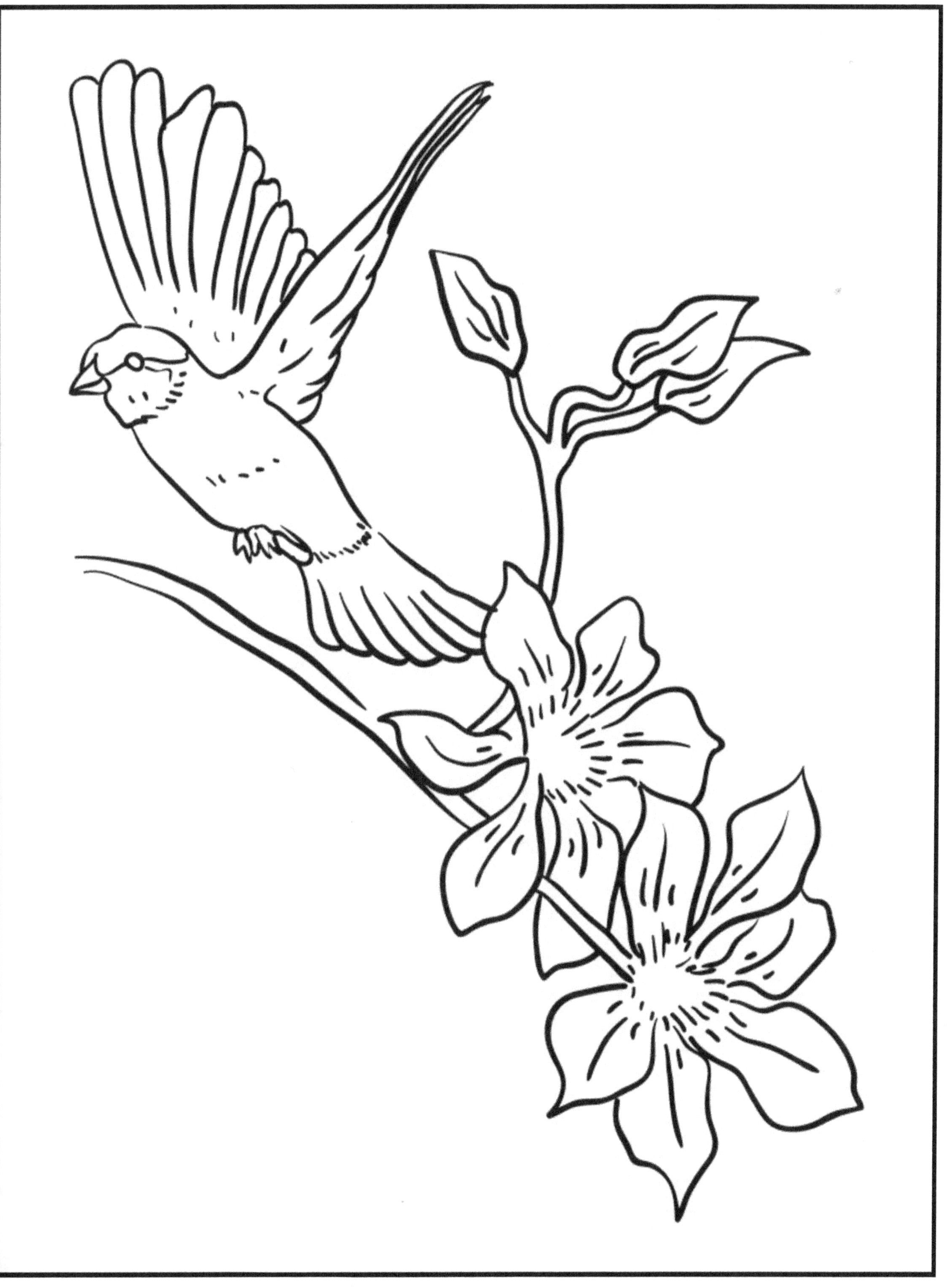

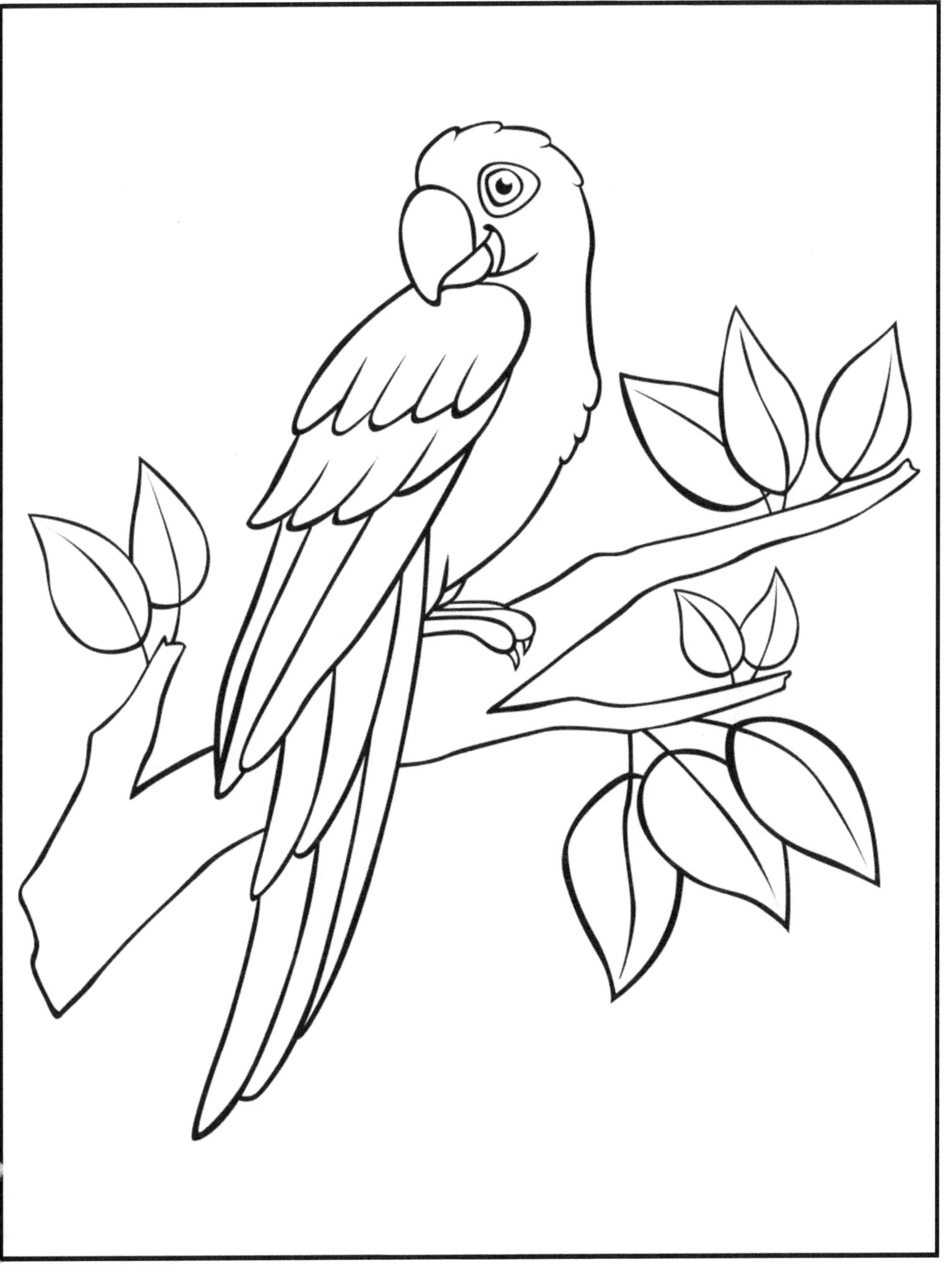

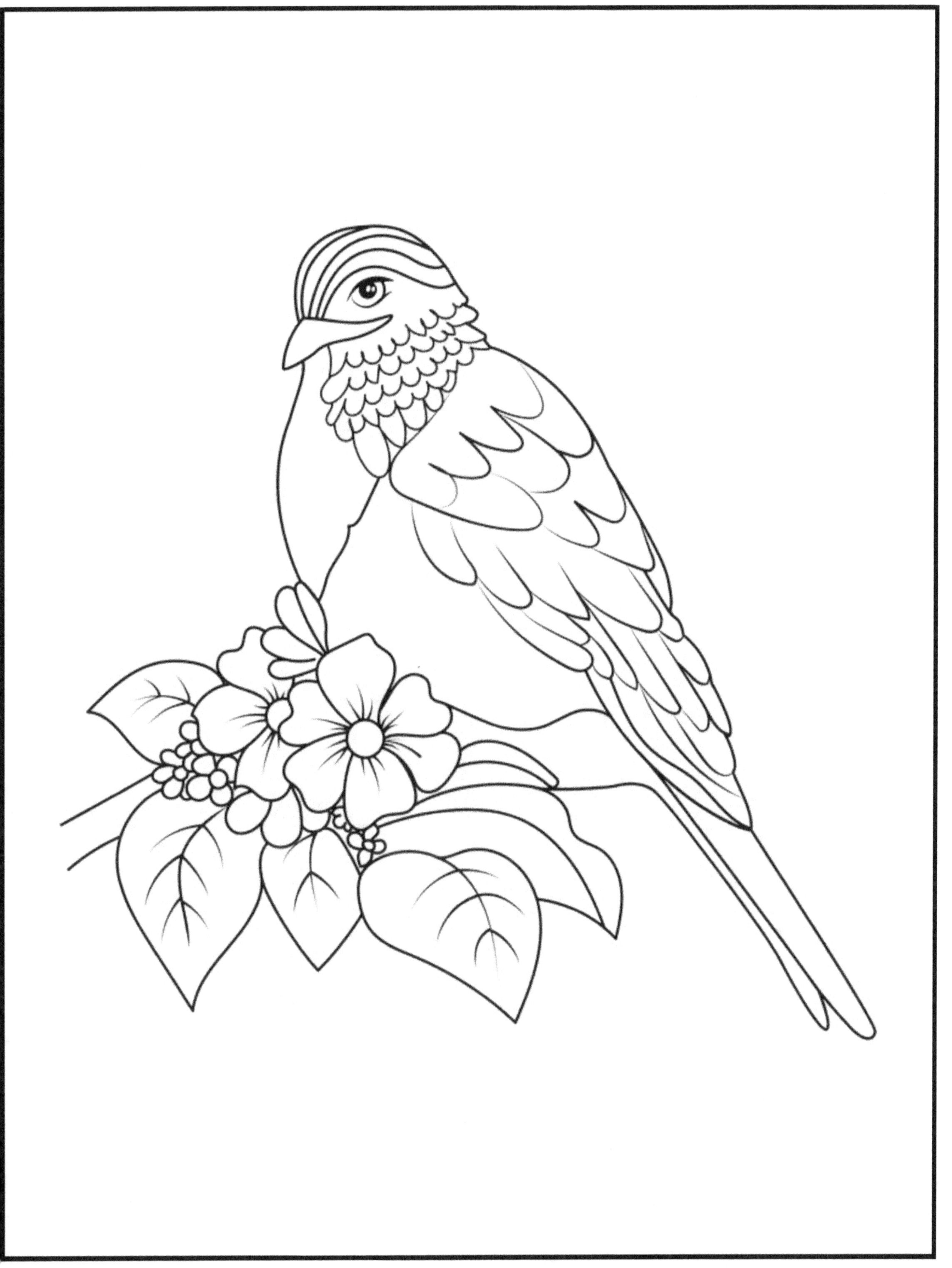

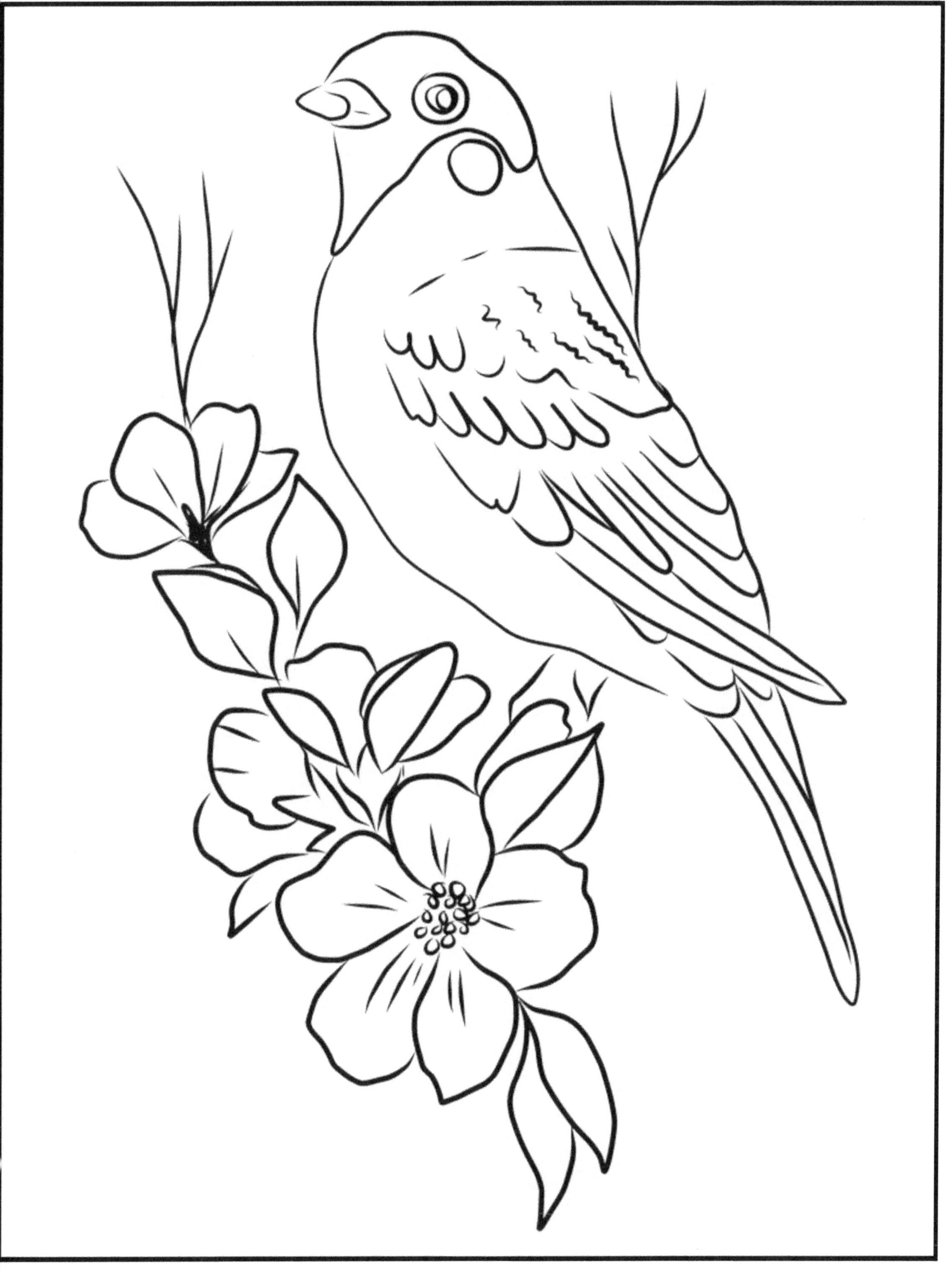

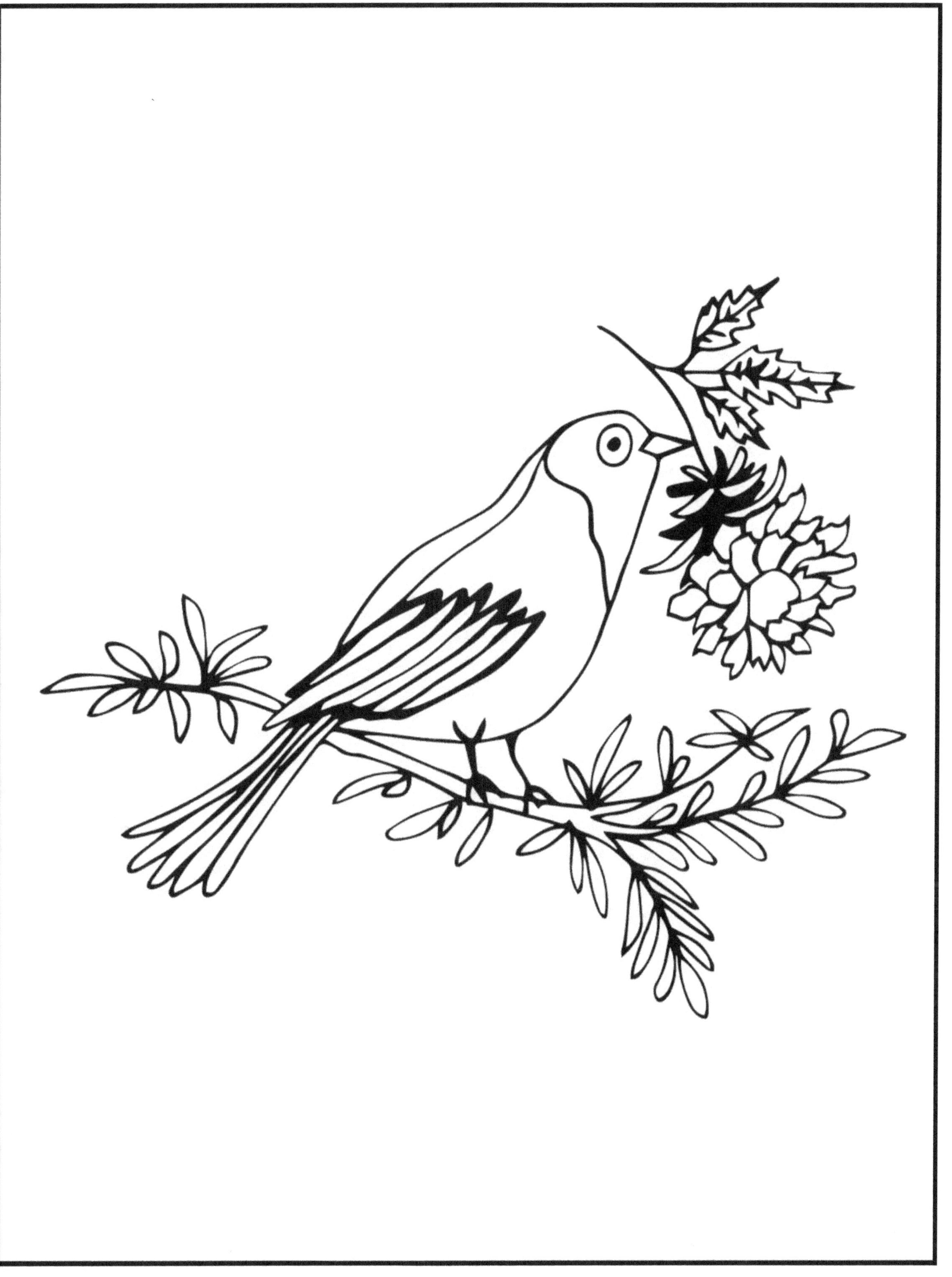

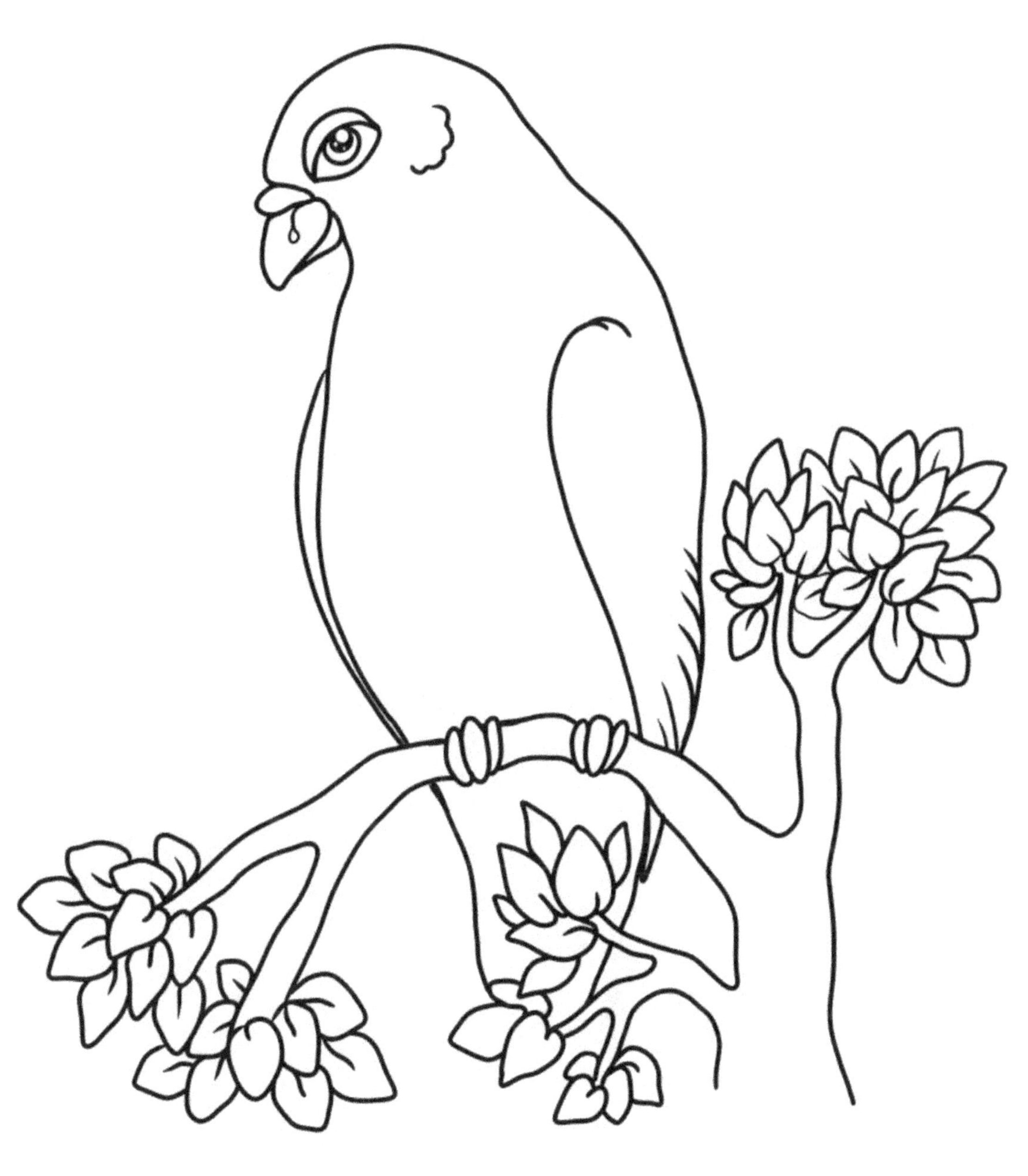

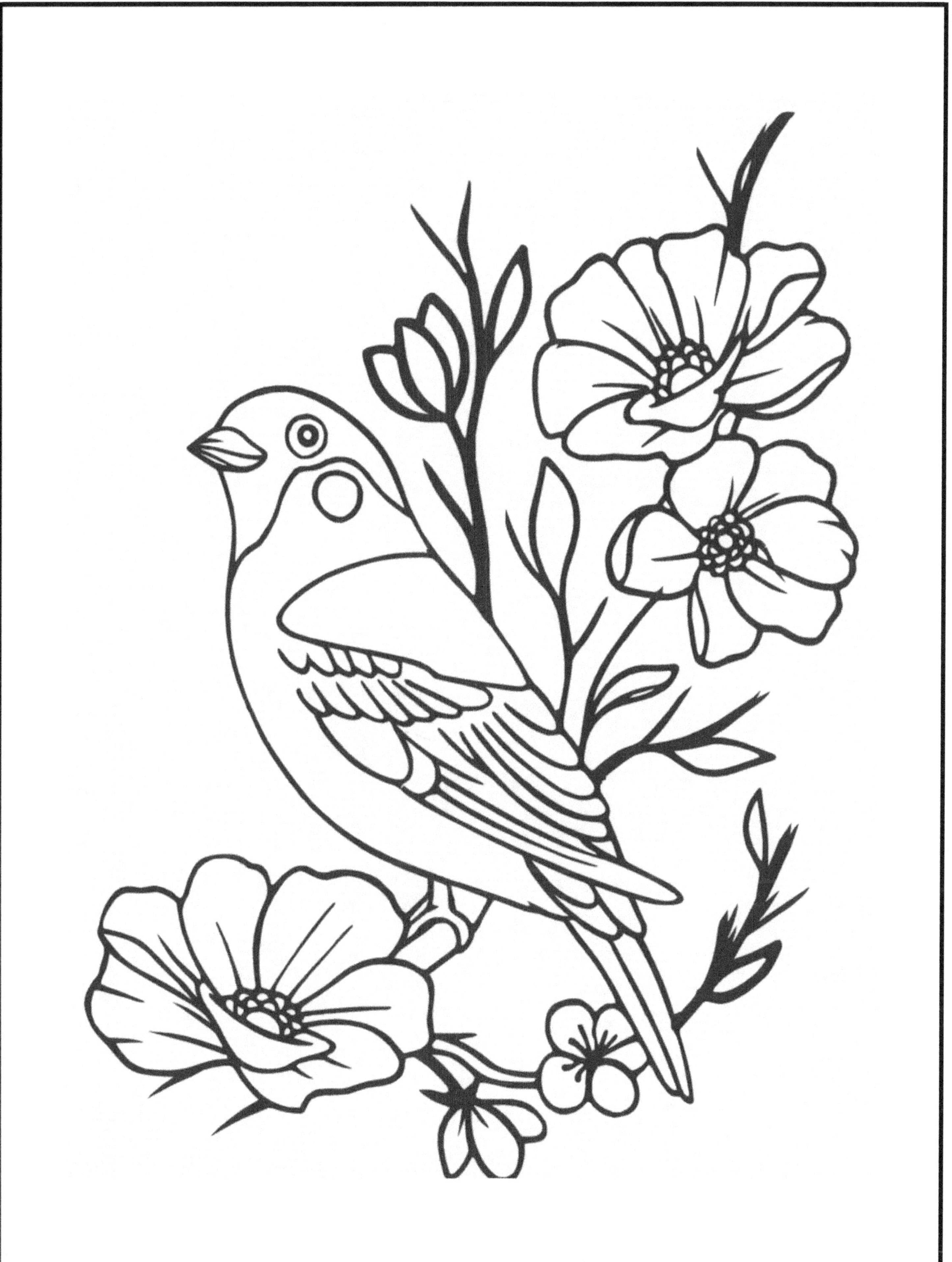

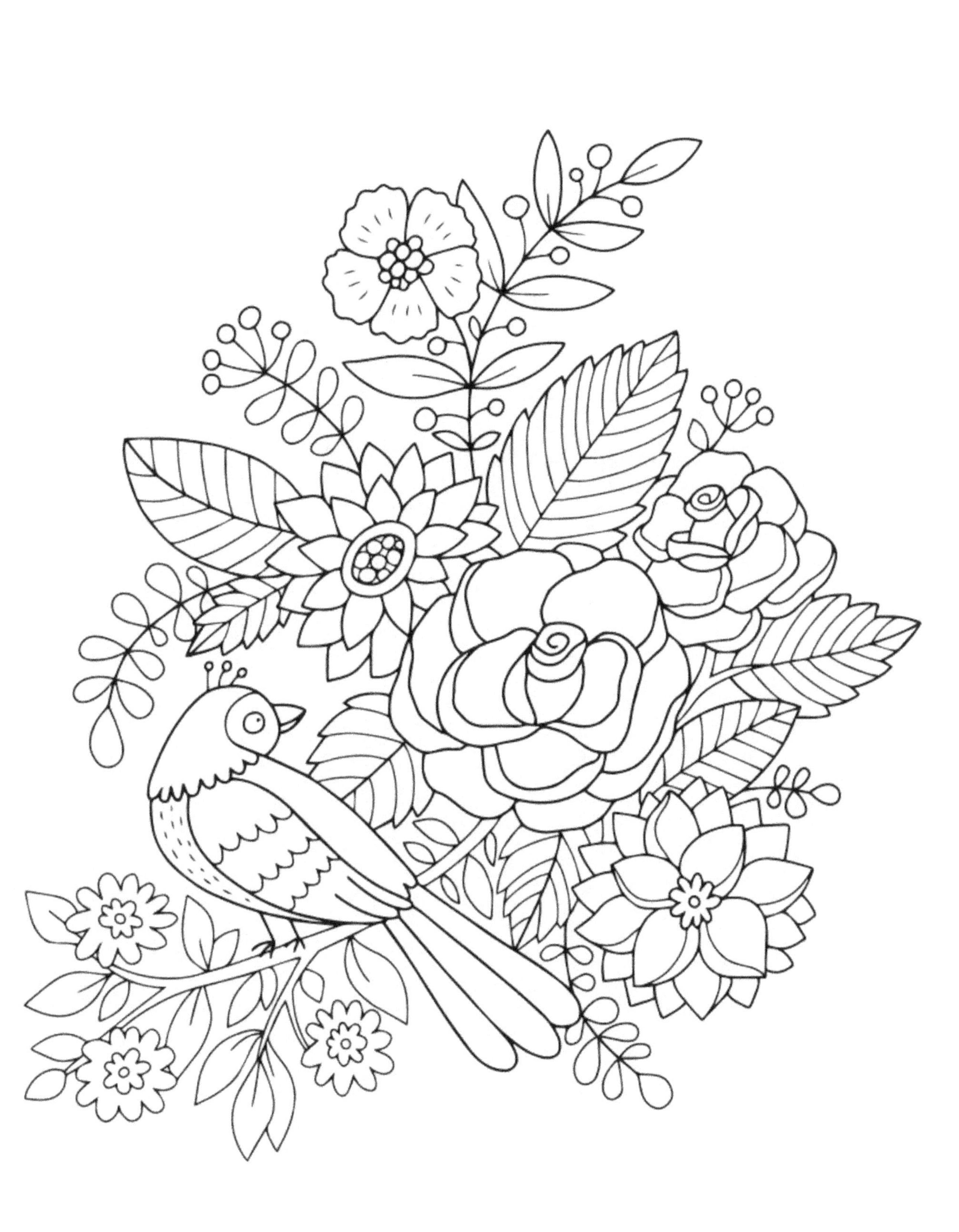

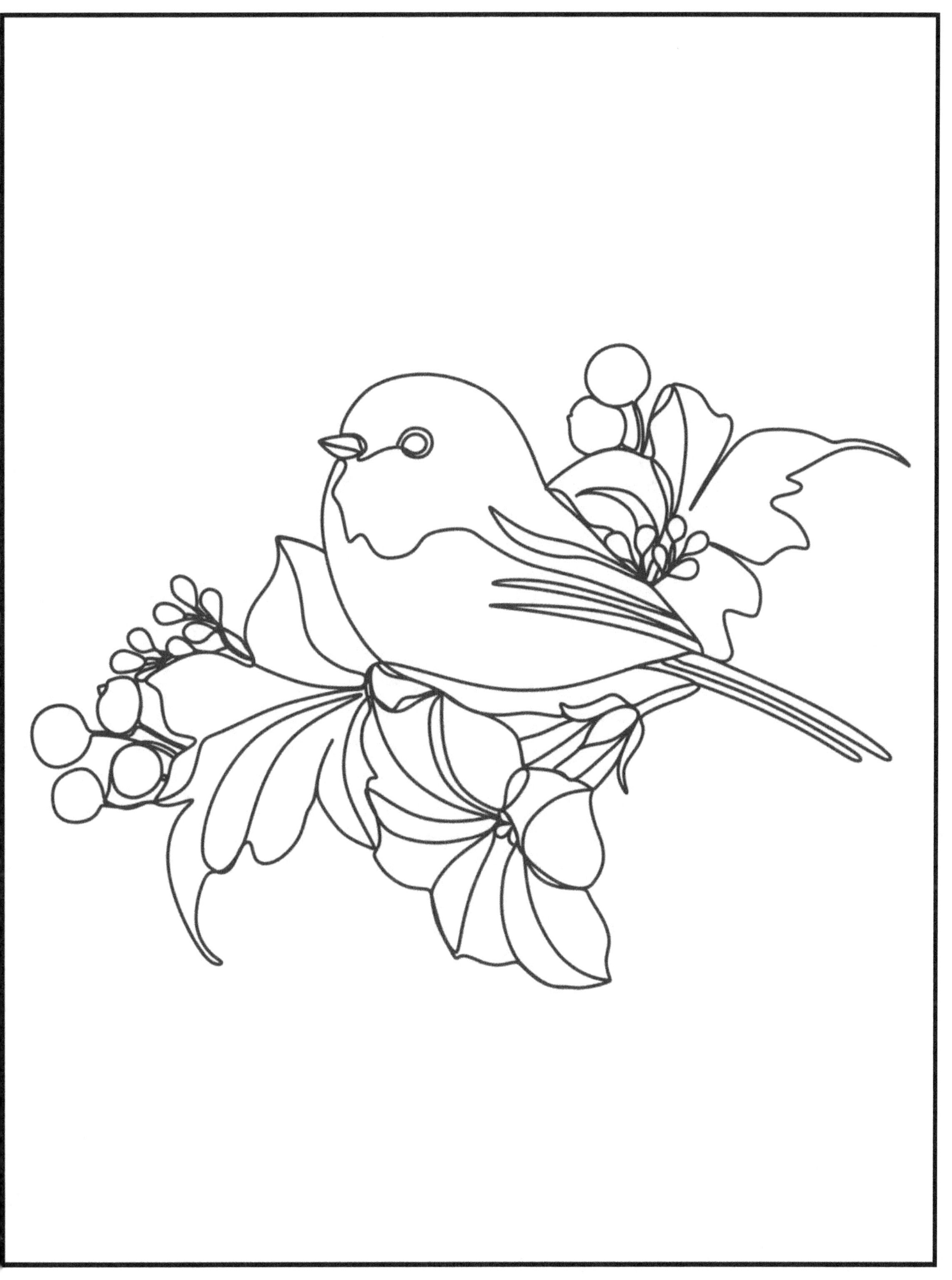

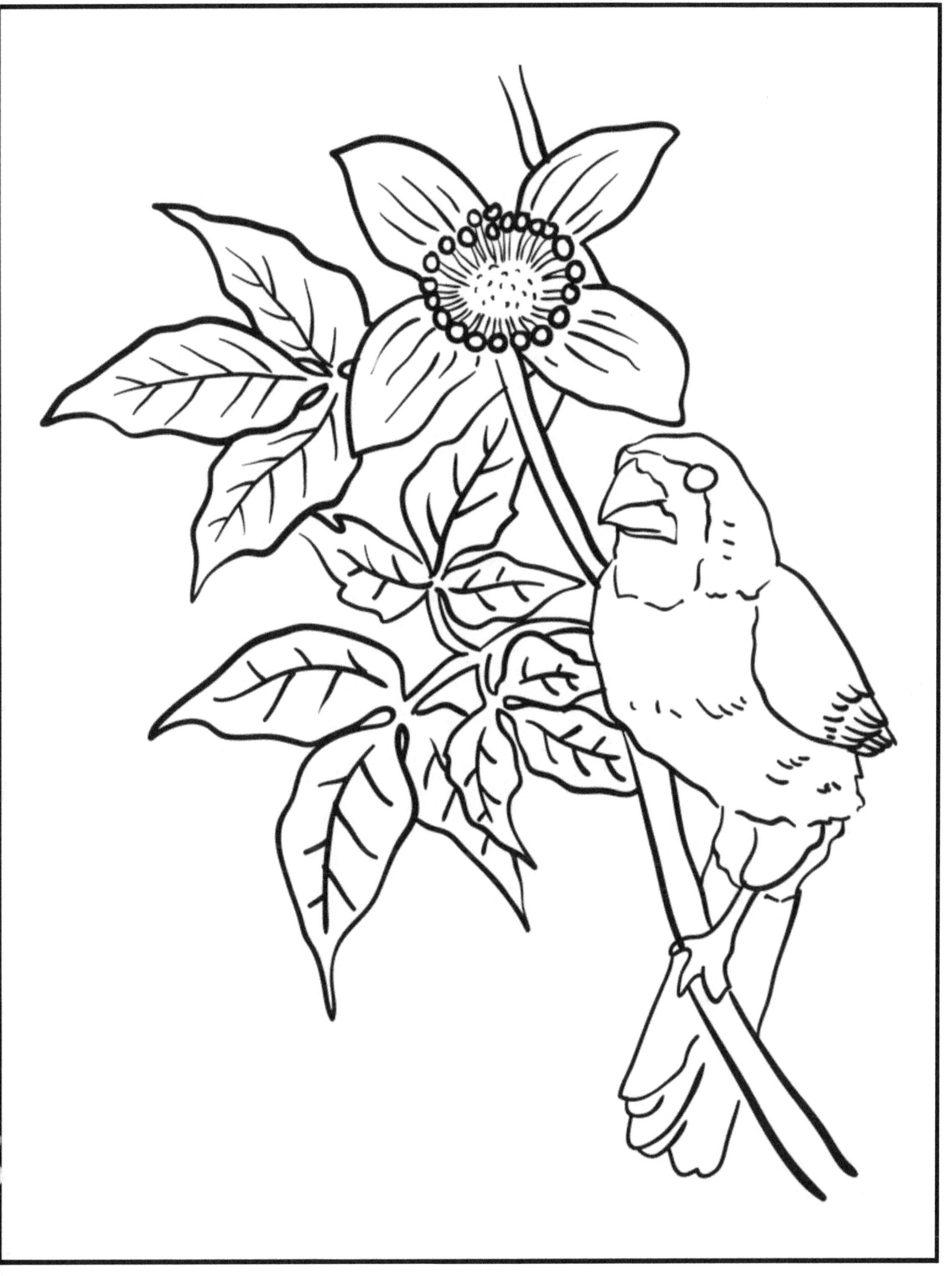

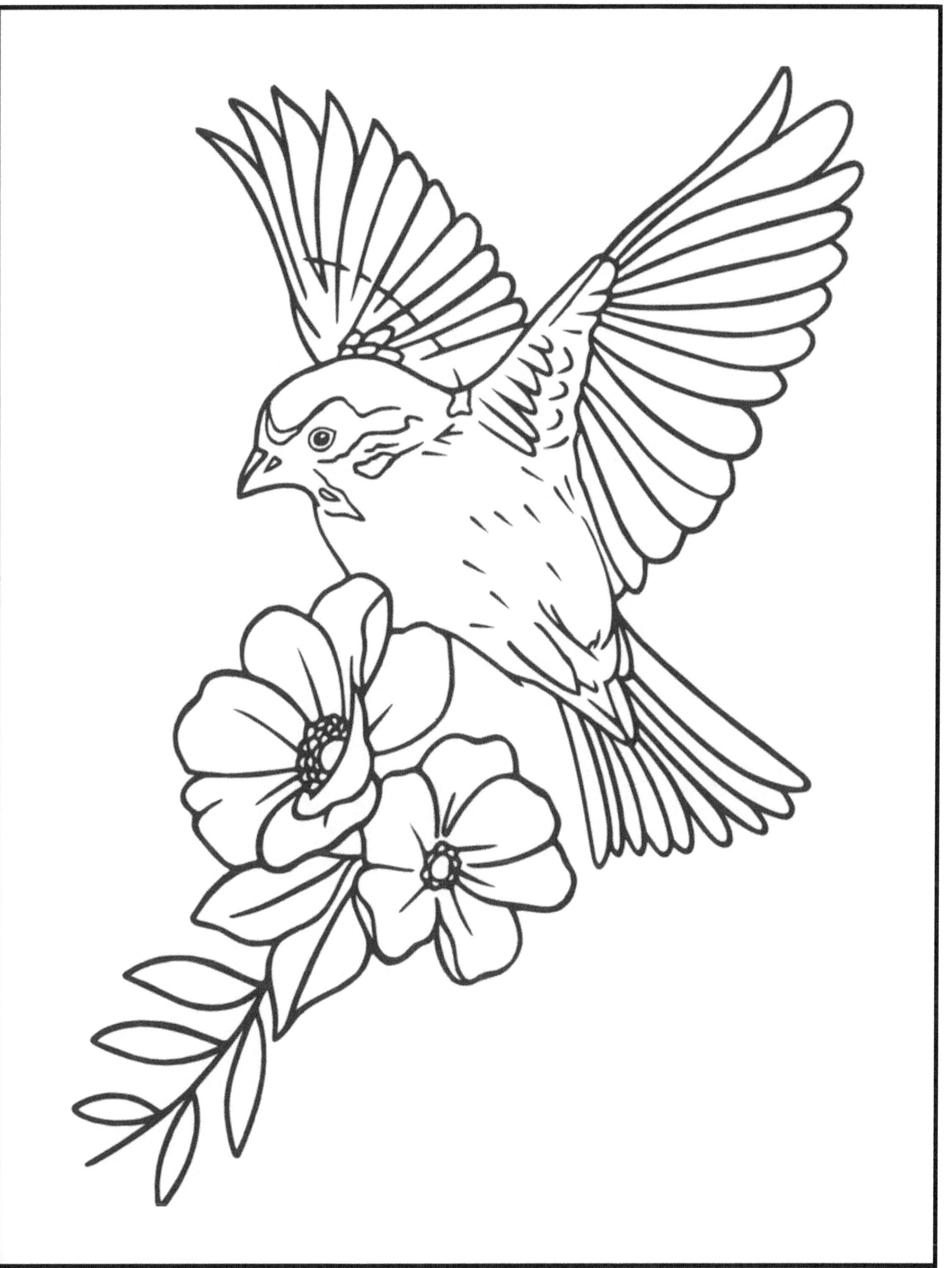

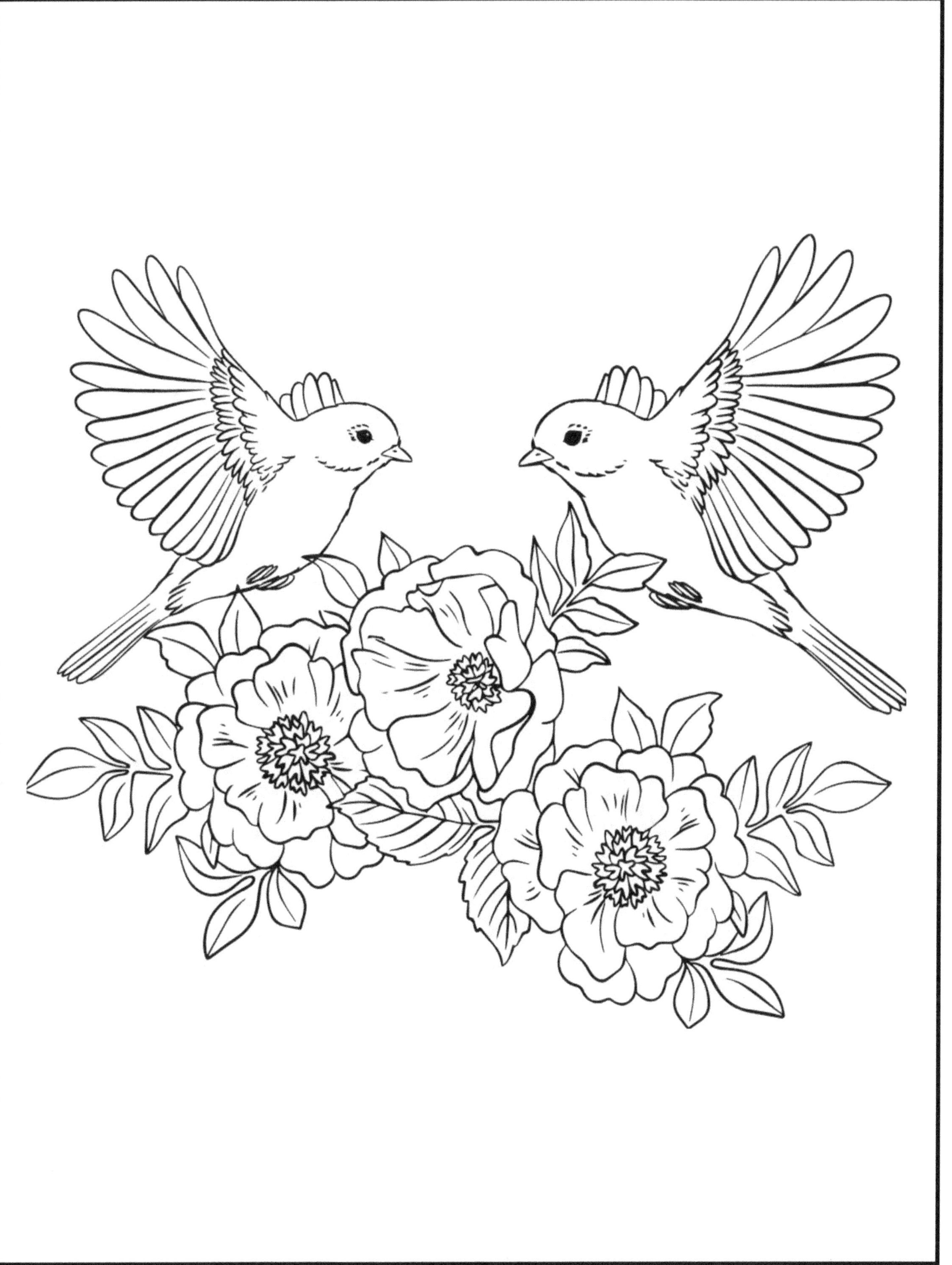

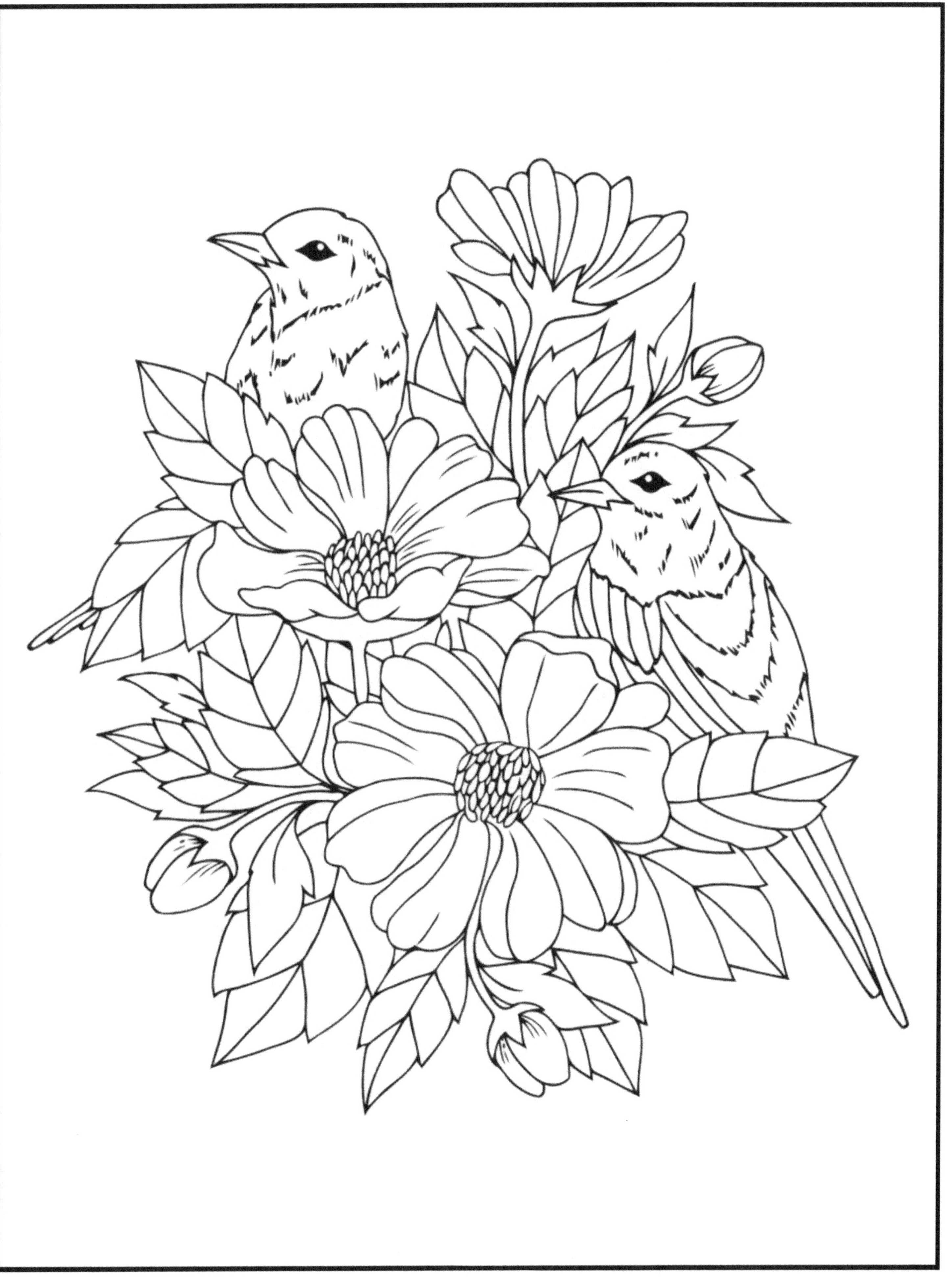

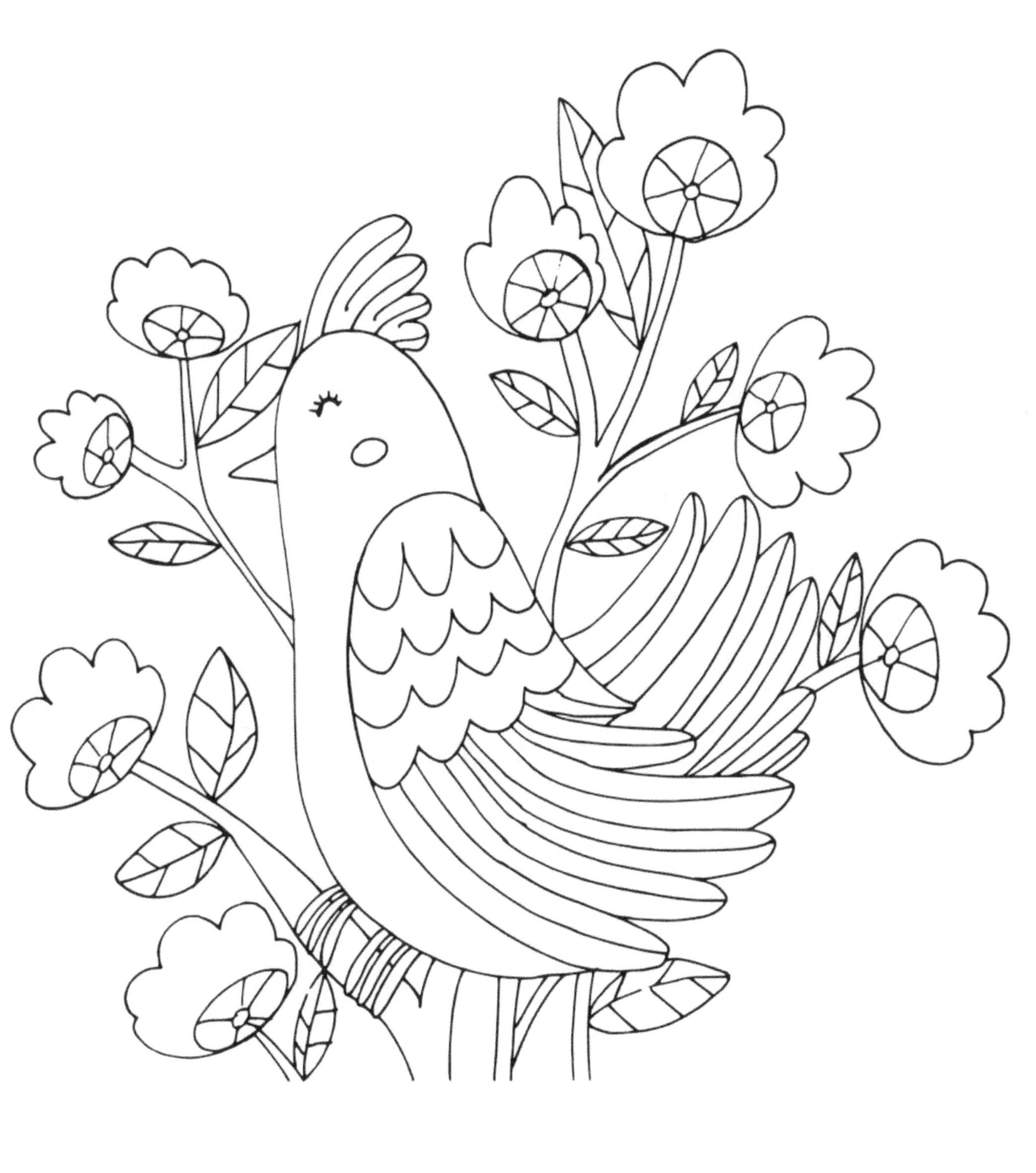

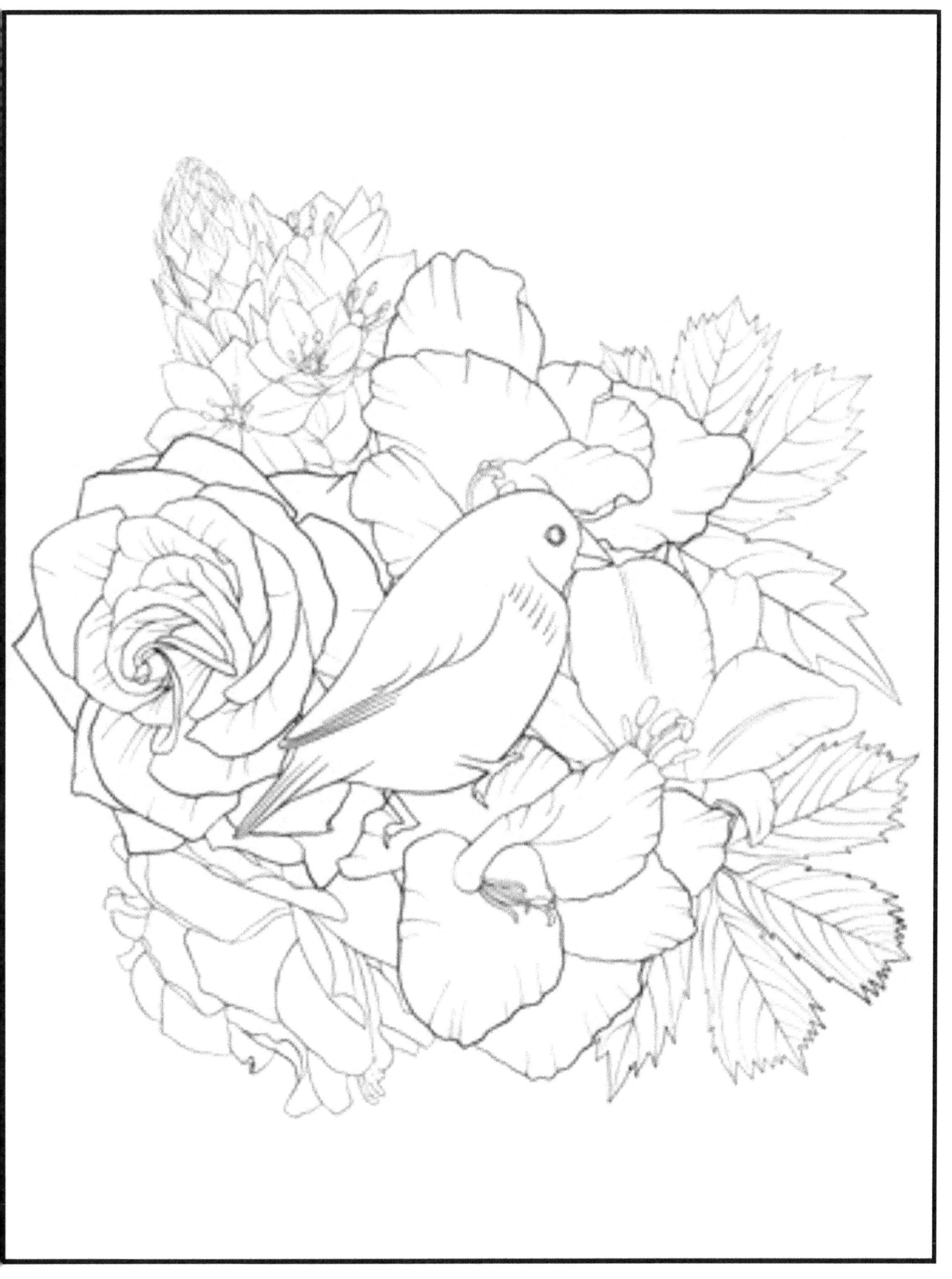

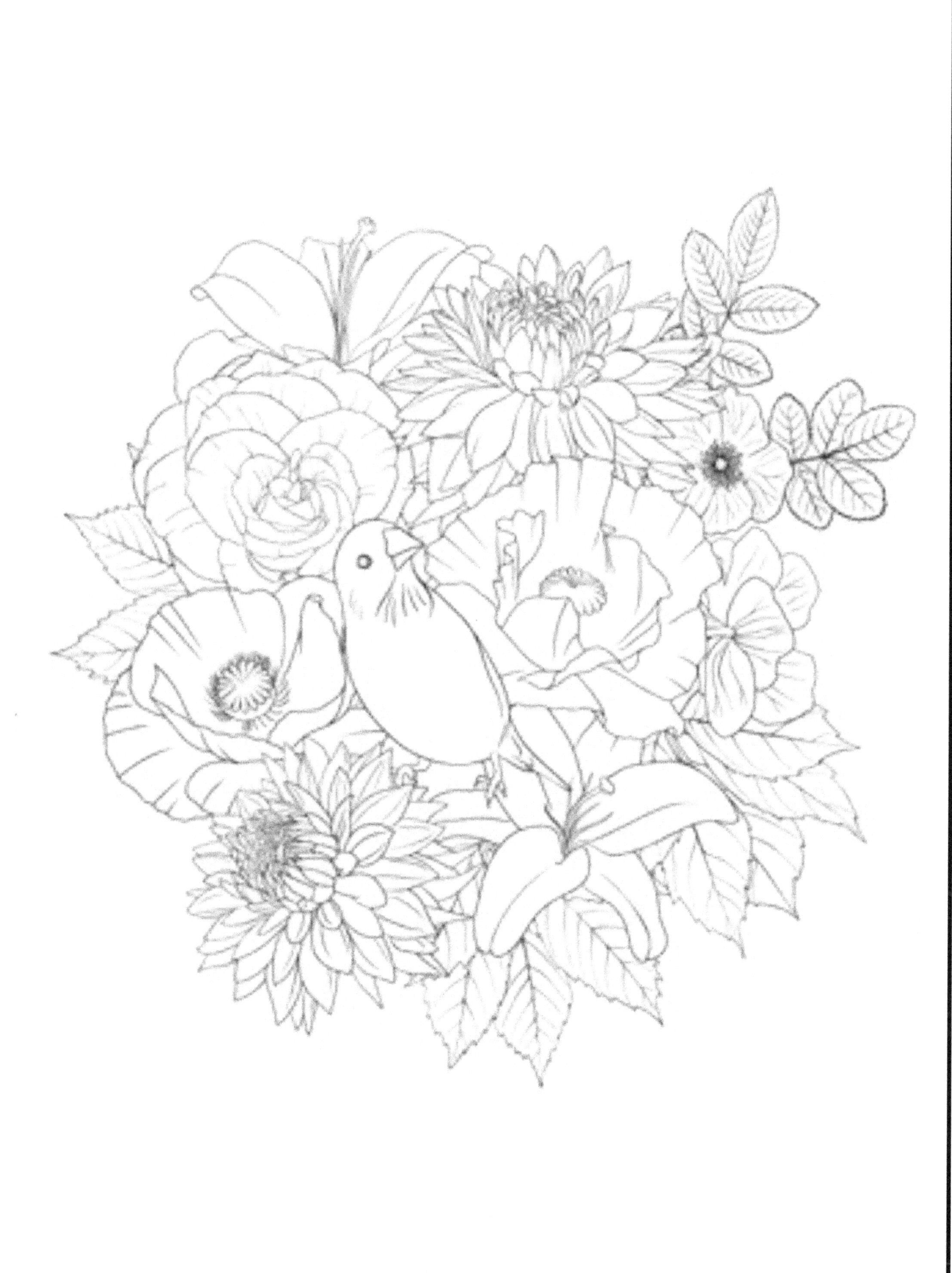

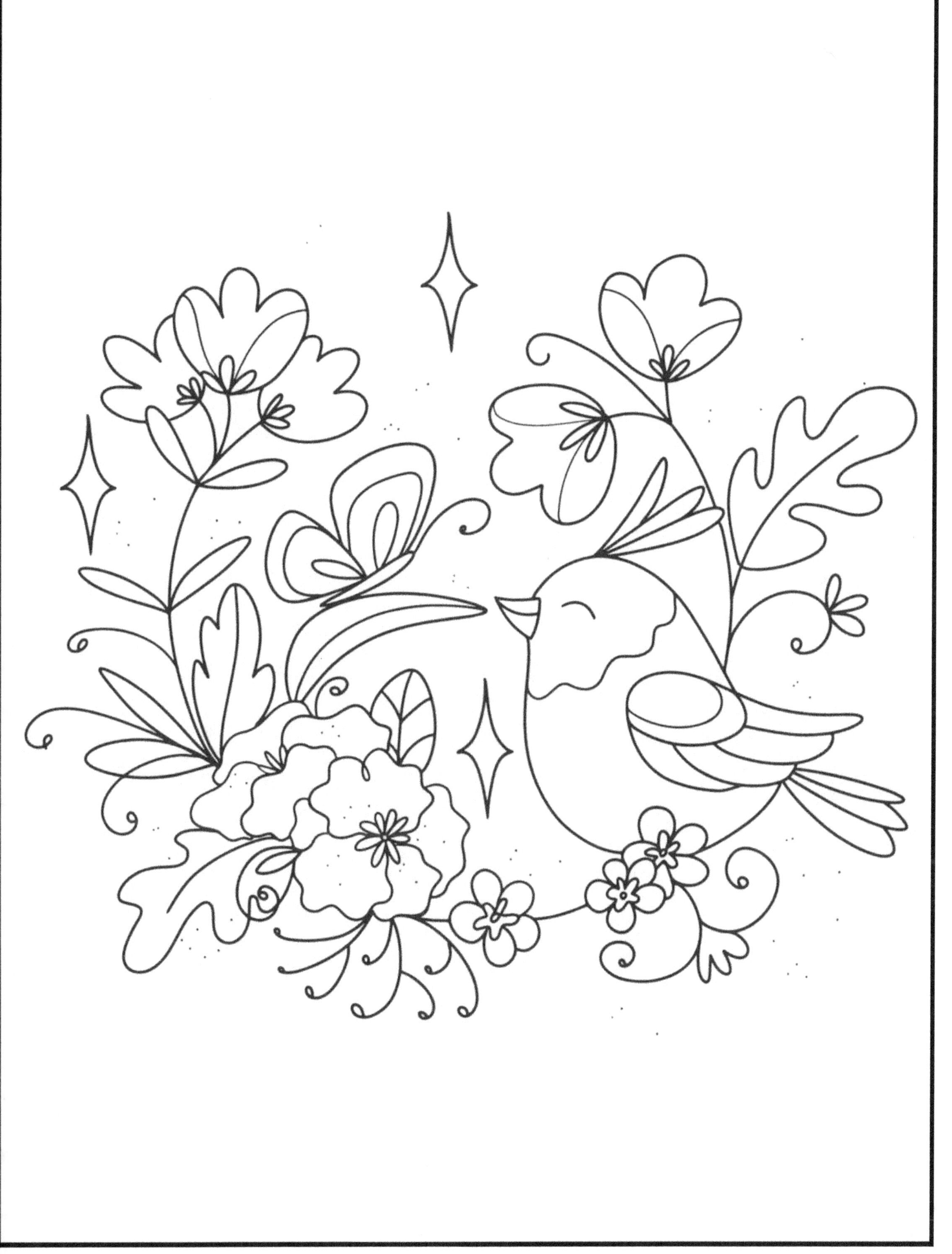

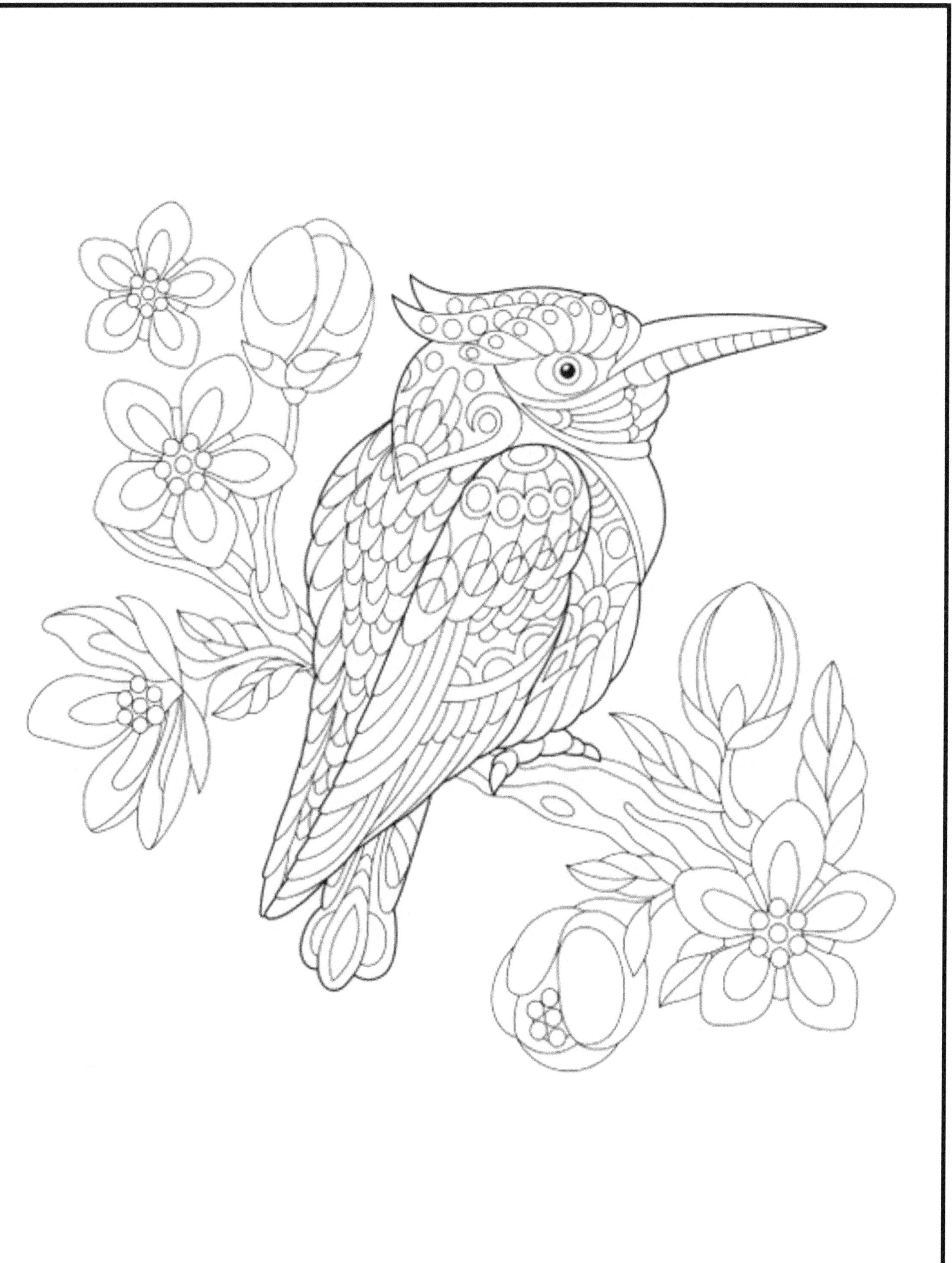

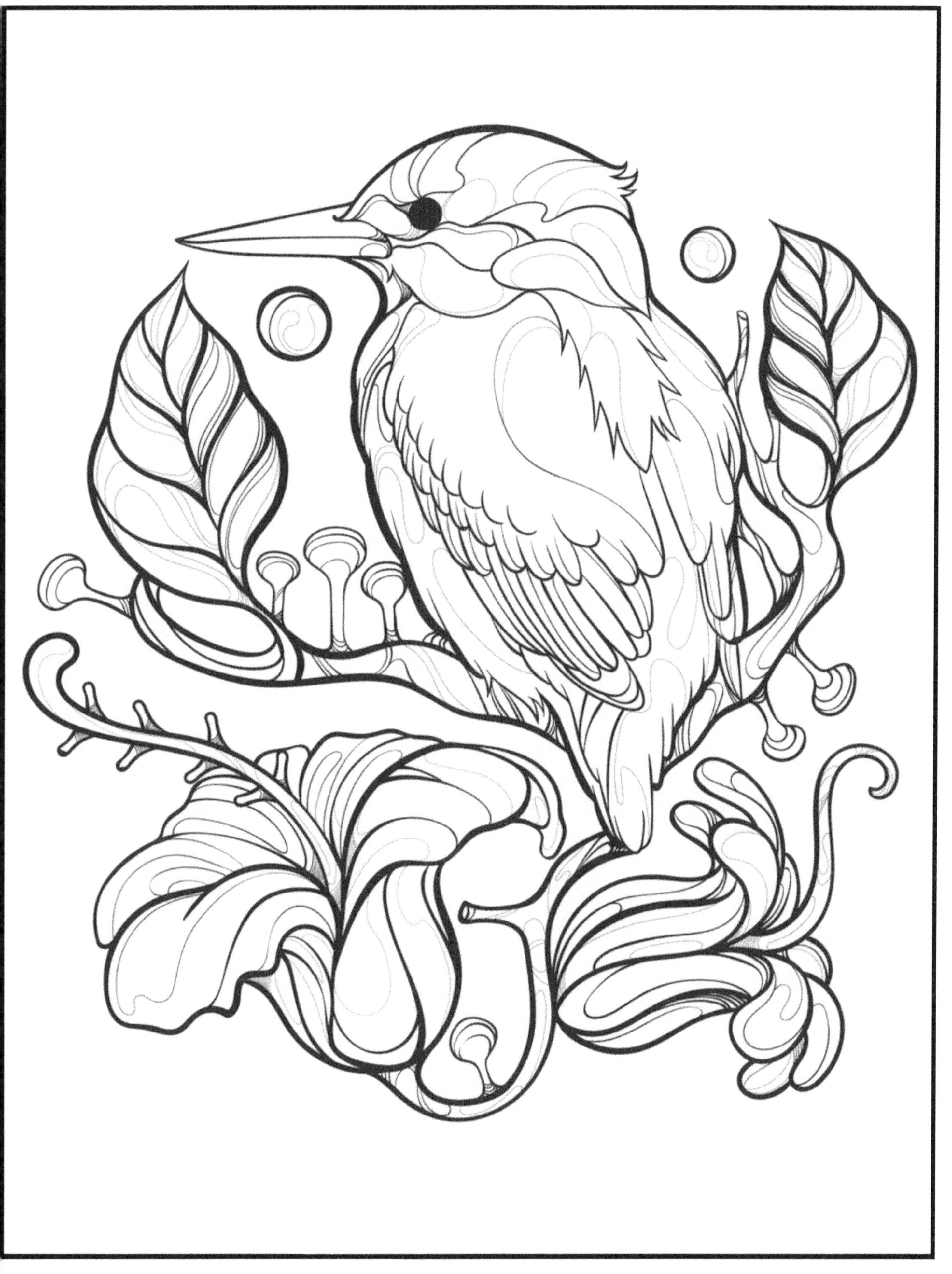

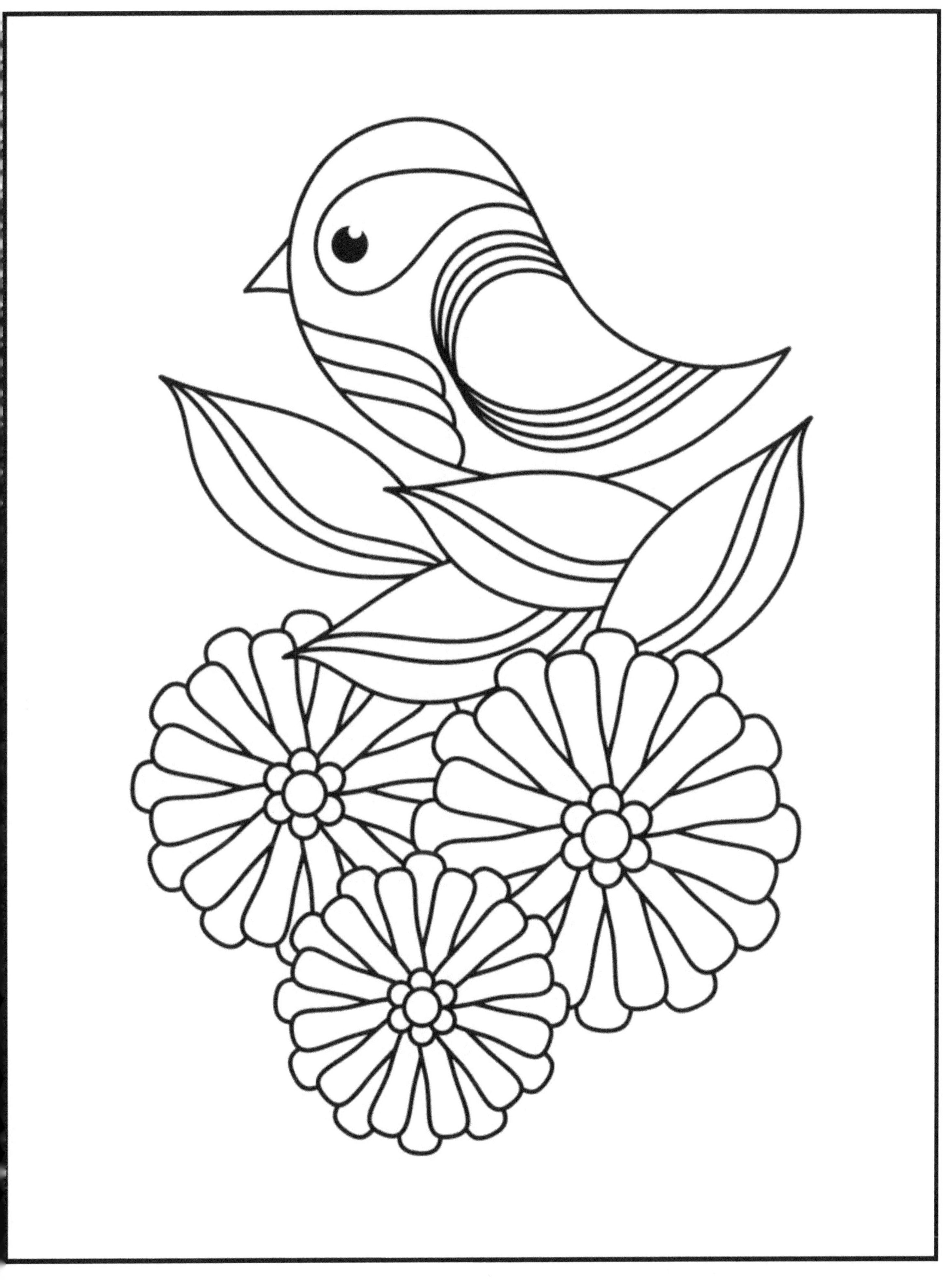

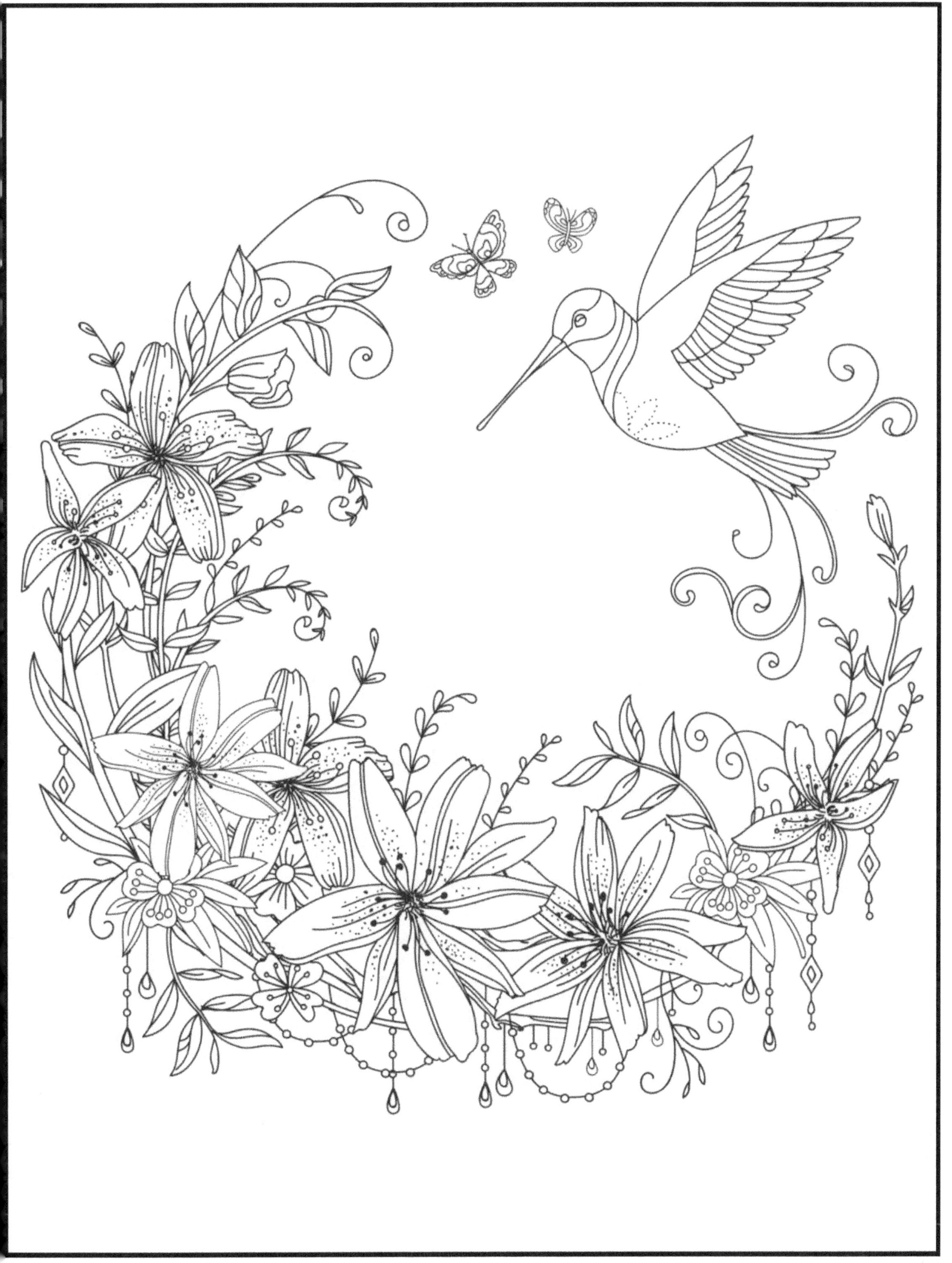

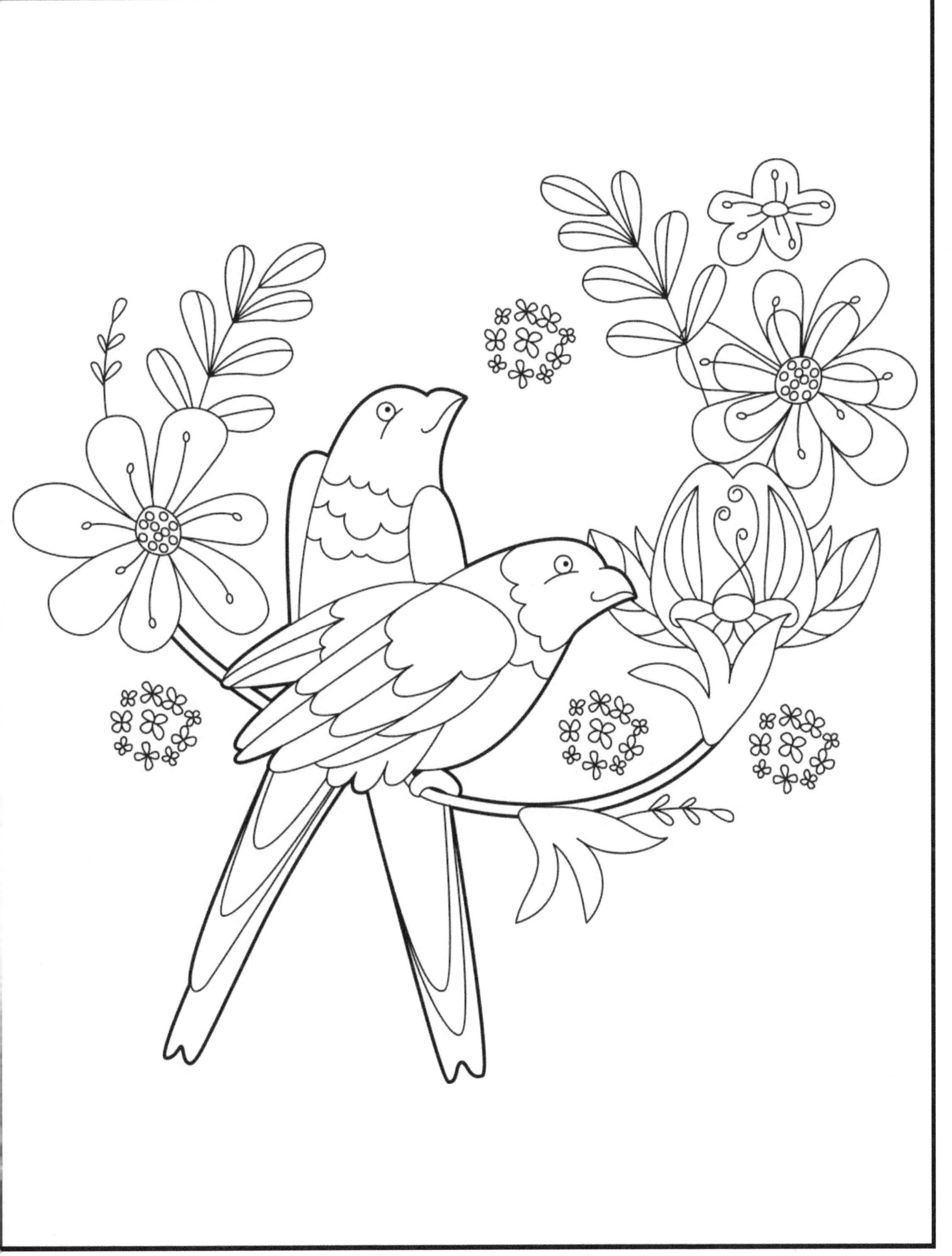

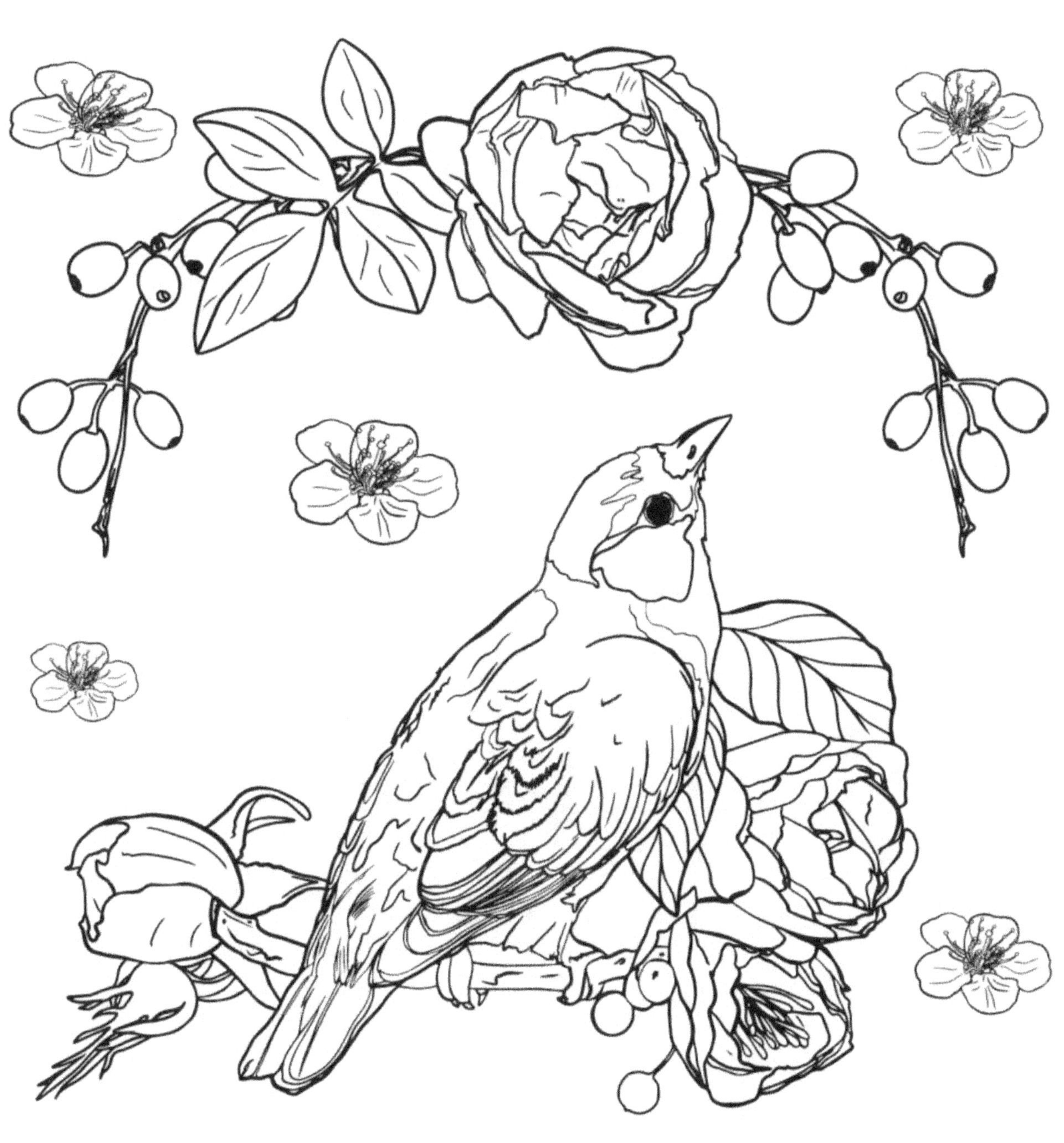

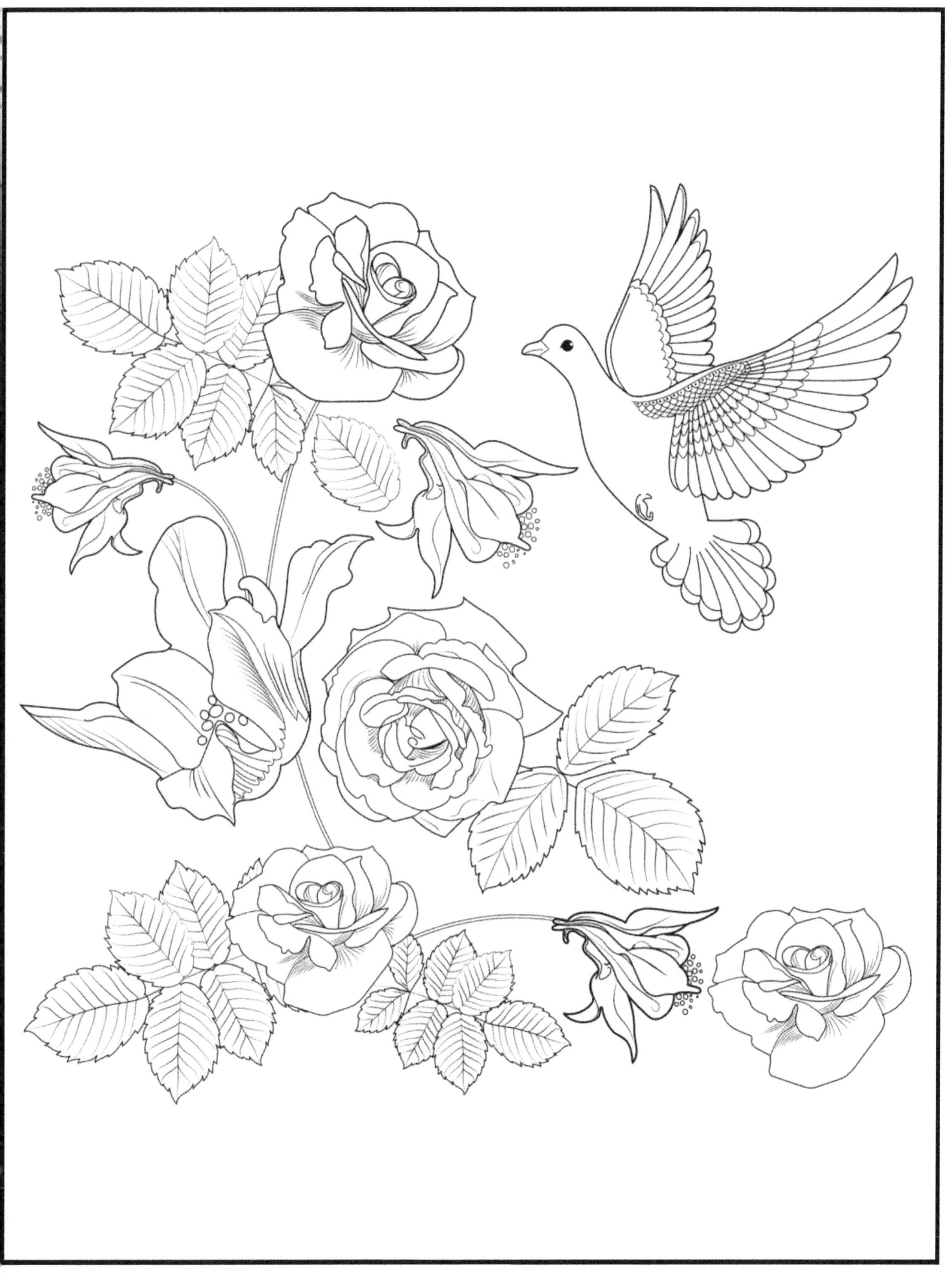

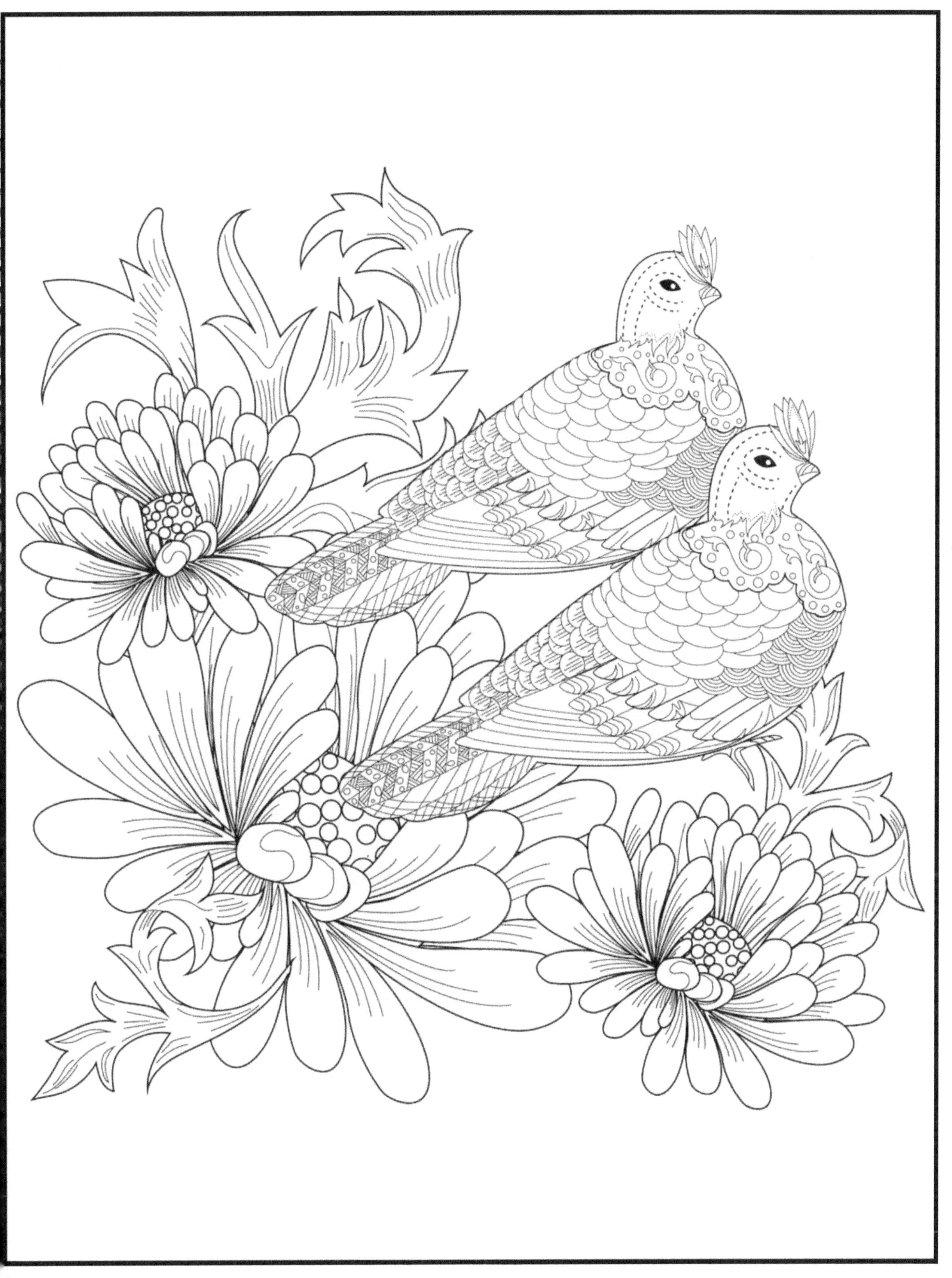

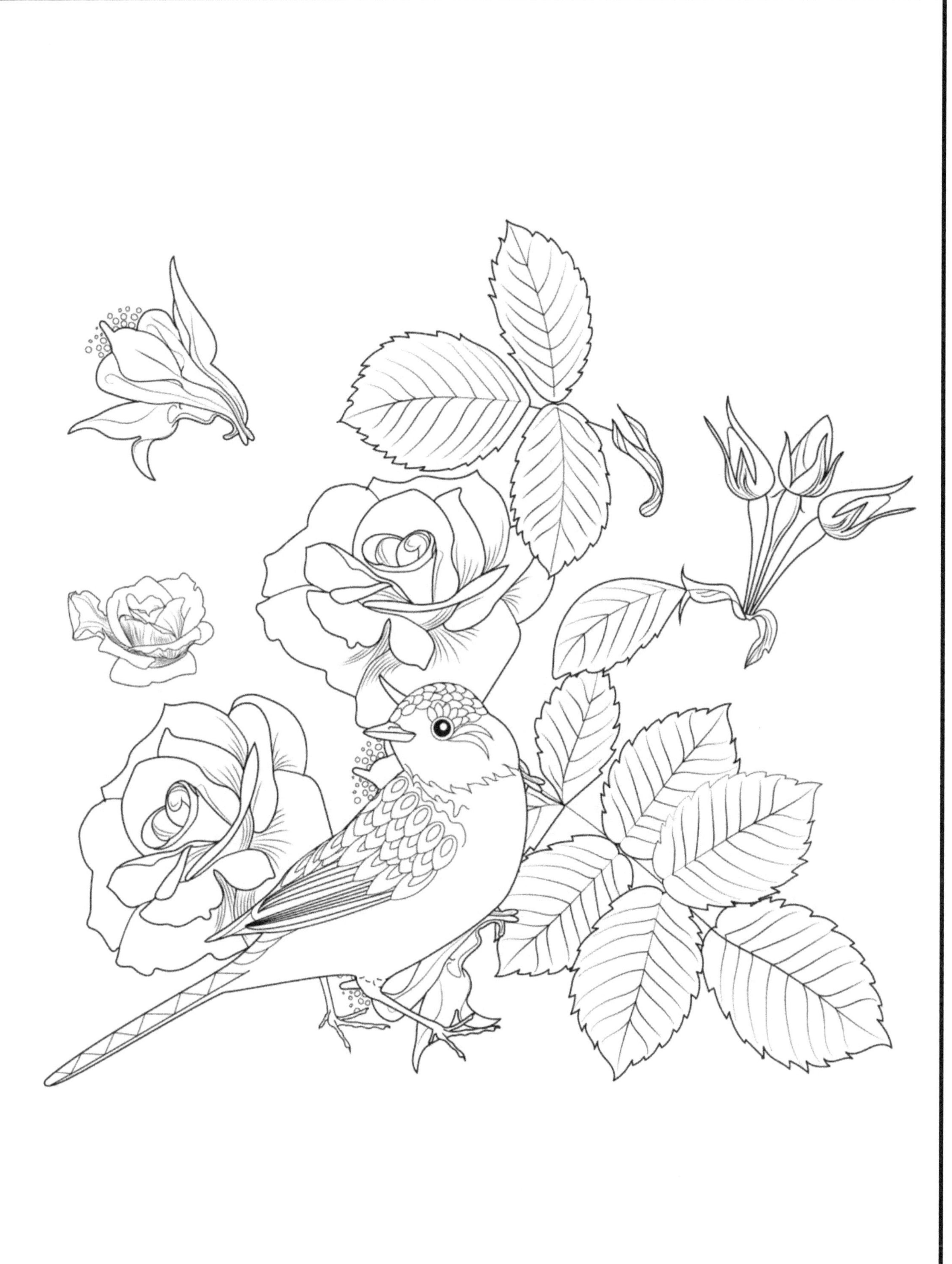